NATURALLY SWEET
BAKING

Carolin Strothe & Sebastian Keitel

NATURALLY SWEET BAKING

Healthier recipes for a guilt-free treat

CONTENTS

Choosing the right recipe   7

Preface by Jamie Oliver   9

Introduction   **10**

Guide to symbols   15

The scent of lilac   **16**

Edible flowers   24

Building blocks: oat muffins   42

From the orchard   **48**

Plums   64

Building blocks: bundt cakes   76

Berries   86

A rich harvest   **112**

Apples   124

Pears   144

Vegetables   152

Fresh from the oven   **156**

Building blocks: banana bread   166

All about baking   **186**

Seasonal calendar   188

Natural colors   190

Basic recipes   192

Baking tips, pans, and conversion table   195

Product knowledge   196

Index   204

Acknowledgments and author biographies   207

Publishing imprint   208

CHOOSING THE RIGHT RECIPE

Recipes for beginners

Strawberry and almond cake — 55
Raspberry and blackberry cobbler — 80
Blueberry galette — 101

Finger foods

Cherry hot cross buns — 31
Strawberry and almond muffins — 38
Red currant teff cookies — 51

Afternoon treats

Teff waffles — 44
Yogurt cake — 63
Apple cake — 127

Quick and easy

Peanut blondies — 41
Apple waffles — 60
Scones — 160

Everyday bliss

Oat muffins — 42
Oat waffles — 82
Fig and walnut bars — 165

Generous baked goods

Spring sheet cake — 52
Plum cake — 119
Quince rye cake — 147

Traditions

Stone fruit crumble — 71
Blueberry pancakes — 85
"Elisenlebkuchen" — 176

Modern classics

Carrot cake — 27
Ricotta cheesecake — 89
Brownies — 168

Old classics

Victoria sponge cake — 59
Blackberry Swiss roll — 102
Pear and walnut bundt cake — 148

Special occasions

Late summer berry gateau — 95
Blueberry naked cake — 107
Cranberry cake — 185

PREFACE

It's with great pleasure that I write the foreword for this beautiful book, created by one of Germany's very own superstar bakers, Carolin Strothe, and her creative genius of a husband, Sebastian Keitel.

I first met Carolin several years ago, when she was one of the many food bloggers and vloggers I got to know on the culinary circuit. I have followed her work ever since on social media, and I can tell you that this chirpy, talented, passionate foodie is definitely the real deal. Carolin lives and breathes good food, and I mean in all areas of cooking, though of course she is particularly skilled in the baking department.

Carolin cherishes the seasonality of ingredients and keeping things natural, and she is a great advocate for local markets, farmers, and producers. In my opinion, she sums up the real fun and joy of contemporary German food.

You'll see from the pictures that her style is steeped in history, embracing the vibrancy and classic look of the swing era, and that sense of heritage is also present in her food. On the one hand, the book is a sumptuous expression of proper German cooking; yet on the other, an experimental, eccentric attitude comes through, and a wonderful curiosity for the rest of the world and its flavors.

This brilliant book is the culmination of the immense creative talent that Carolin and Sebastian share between them. Their joy for food, music, and dance and their eye for design, photography, and color just makes life that little bit brighter, and you'll experience that yourself as you flip through this book. Just like all of Carolin's recipes, when I see these gorgeous photographs, I want to tuck in immediately. I often want to eat my phone when she posts something new on Instagram. (And if you're not already following her, what are you waiting for?!)

WHEN I SEE THESE GORGEOUS PHOTOS, I WANT TO TUCK IN IMMEDIATELY.

The incredible baked goods here are deliciously indulgent and tasty, but also designed to cut back on sugar. Baking is never going to be healthy, but Carolin strives to adopt a healthier approach in the creation of her recipes, and they don't disappoint. The celebration of ingredients and flavors is fantastic. I know this book will live happily in your home and be used often—and hopefully passed on to future generations. Enjoy it, and happy baking!

Jamie Oliver

INTRODUCTION

Why we are writing this book

We both associate childhood very strongly with special, carefree times spent outside in the garden. We enjoyed wonderful experiences, such as eating fruit from the berry bushes in summer and, in the fall, gathering up old apple varieties, picking juicy pears, or collecting mushrooms in the woods. From an early age, we learned from our parents and grandparents when each kind of fruit and vegetable was in season and how they could be used in cooking and baking. During the weekend, a delicious cake would invariably be baked using freshly harvested fruit from the garden, so our intimate connection to nature began pretty much from birth. Nowadays, we still love to unwind from the hustle and bustle of everyday life by baking timeless classic cakes at the weekend or by giving them a new interpretation and enjoying the results with family and friends.

FROM AN EARLY AGE, WE LEARNED ... WHEN EACH KIND OF FRUIT AND VEGETABLE WAS IN SEASON.

The health aspect of cooking also plays a big role in our recipes. As we grow older and our daily lives become more stressful, naturally we become more interested in our bodies and general health. This interest links to the topic of nutrition and its significant impact on our well-being. We have been focused on using natural ingredients in our food for over 15 years now, so eating healthy has become second nature and doesn't feel like an effort.

Once you begin to look more closely into nutrition, it soon becomes clear that the highly processed foods that are so ubiquitous are not only deficient in terms of natural ingredients, they also foster an unhealthy diet. According to a 2016 survey by ReportLinker, only 36 percent of Americans cook and eat at home daily. Shared meals are no longer an integral part of our daily routine, as we eat at home far less often. Instead, people often grab food while they are on the move, eating when they happen to see something that looks delicious or simply to fulfill a craving. In a dynamic world—where the key preoccupations are work, stress, or leisure activities—the motto is "quick and easy." Many kids no longer learn how to cook from scratch. In the past, girls were taught how to cook in home economics, or grandmothers passed on their knowledge to the next generation. Today, too often, this knowledge isn't passed on.

And yet the natural world continues to provide a diverse and rich cornucopia of ingredients that are incomparable when it comes to flavor. All too often, ingredients are gradually being forgotten thanks to industrial-scale mass production. For understandable reasons, industrial production focuses on the ingredients that are easiest to use and which can be processed most efficiently to generate the largest revenues. High quantities of sugar and fat are often added to conceal the substandard quality of other ingredients. This situation is what prompted us to design and write this book. We want to restore our relationship with natural ingredients. Of course, there's an element of nostalgia involved, too. But, most importantly, it has become very clear that we are harming ourselves and exploiting our planet

with our current lifestyle, sometimes with disastrous and incalculable consequences. We would like our book to make a contribution (however small) to changing this.

Why we love sweet things

Have you ever tried to buy a jar of sour cherries without added sugar? It's really hard. Sugar is everywhere, concealed and unconcealed. It's a predicament: too much sugar is unhealthy, yet we love it. And no wonder—after all, we get our first taste of sugar from our mother's milk. Along with fat and protein, breast milk primarily contains the disaccharide lactose, which is what gives the milk its sweet taste. The reason we cannot resist sweet foods is due to a primal survival instinct. Sweet things are equated with goodness; we've sensed it in our bones from time immemorial. Our Stone Age ancestors were far more reliant on this sense of taste than we are today. Deciding whether to swallow something or spit it out was absolutely crucial to their survival. Their sense of taste functioned almost as a chemical sensor for the quality of different foods. Poisonous plants often taste bitter, and acidic flavors can indicate that something

isn't ripe yet or that it is contaminated with bacteria. A "sweet" flavor, on the other hand, has positive associations. In particular, it serves as an indicator of high nutrient density. This was of immense importance to our prehistoric ancestors because they could never be sure when they would be getting their next meal or when they might experience a period of famine. So the human addiction to sugar is entirely natural from an evolutionary perspective and is the consequence of thousands of years of scarcity.

Apart from honey, food and drink with high levels of added sugar didn't appear in our diets until relatively recently. It was only when the industrial mass production of food took off that an excess of sweet dishes arose. A recent study found that many in the US consume more than the daily recommended amount of sugar. This includes sugars added to food, as well as those that occur naturally, say, in honey and fruit juice. Experts all agree that too much sugar is being eaten. Poor diets combined with lack of exercise have seen a rise in so-called lifestyle conditions such as type 2 diabetes and obesity. As a result, in its new guidelines, the WHO (World Health Organization) has reduced the recommended daily intake of sugar to a maximum of 2 tablespoons.

If you read the ingredients lists on food packaging in more detail, you will quickly realize that it is almost impossible to buy packaged or processed foods or convenience goods without filling your shopping basket with additional sugar. Clearly, it is crucial to regain control over our own sugar consumption and to handle sugar with more restraint. But how? The best way is to get into the kitchen and start cooking and baking yourself. That's the only way you can really control how much sugar, fat, and salt actually goes into your food. If you also use as many natural ingredients as possible, you will be well on your way to a healthy, pleasurable diet.

Sugar makes us happy because it triggers a response from the reward center in our brain. On the other hand, sugar also makes you tired because there is an inevitable energy slump after the initial sugar high thanks to the way it causes our blood sugar levels to go up and down. The body then demands more sugar, and so the cycle begins, and we end up consuming sugar without even noticing. Sugar is concealed in countless foods in the form of so-called empty carbohydrates—for example, in white flour. Often it is also combined with high quantities of saturated fats. One thing is absolutely clear: ultimately, sugar is always sugar. It doesn't matter whether it is packaged as a soft drink, or as agave syrup, or whether you go back to natural sugars in the form of fruit (= fructose). Anything ending in "ose" contains sugar. So the solution is not just to use different sugars, but ideally also to use less.

The transition away from consuming high levels of refined sugar is a process that requires some adjustment. If you are used to eating lots of sugar, anything containing less sugar will initially taste strange. But by abstaining from refined sugars and products containing sugar for just 1–2 weeks, you will find your sensitivity to flavor increases very rapidly, and you will be amazed just how sweet and "harsh" sugar tastes and how little of it you actually need. By following this approach, you will come to appreciate and recognize natural aromas and flavors. Sugars and sweeteners are not the only substances that taste sweet. For instance, cinnamon can also convey an impression of sweetness. And some natural ingredients, such as strawberries, taste inherently sweet. In fact, every variety of strawberry tastes fundamentally different.

MANY FRUIT VARIETIES TODAY ARE CULTIVATED SPECIFICALLY TO TASTE SWEETER.

Many fruit varieties today are cultivated specifically to taste sweeter. Apples, for instance, have been cultivated to remove polyphenols (see page 200). As a result, modern apple varieties taste sweet but are otherwise singularly lacking in flavor. Sweetness cannot be a substitute for flavor.

Nonetheless, enjoyable baking is impossible without sugar, so we don't renounce it completely. As advocates of diversity, we use types of sugar that differ from the classic, white processed variety. Sugars such as dark brown sugar do not taste as aggressively sweet and have an interesting flavor of their own. Dark brown sugar is less processed and still contains certain minerals. We also use as little sugar as possible for our recipes. As Paracelsus once said, "All things are poison and nothing is without poison; only the dose makes a thing not a poison."

Back to our roots

There are many arguments for using more wholesome and natural ingredients. In baking, not only will you benefit from high-quality nutrients and fiber, your cakes will also have far more exciting flavors and textures. White flour and sugar are rather lacking in flavor on their own. Whole-grain flours and ancient grain varieties, on the other hand, taste earthy, diverse, and nutty. Even smaller quantities can be enough to make you feel full and content.

Ancient grain varieties include heritage spelt, einkorn (see page 196), emmer (see page 197), rye, and pseudo-grains such as buckwheat (see page 196) or teff (see page 197). Archaeological artifacts from around the time 10,000 BCE prove that the cultivation of ancient grains has a long history. Einkorn and emmer, for instance, were first grown in the Middle East before spreading to Europe. Hildegard von Bingen (1098–1179) wrote enthusiastically about spelt in a number of different texts. And even at the start of the 19th century, spelt (see page 196) was the most widely cultivated grain in central Europe. However, wheat varieties with higher yields began to replace it and gradually took over more and more of the crop-growing areas, until spelt fell almost completely into oblivion. Happily, it is currently experiencing something of a comeback, because spelt has excellent baking properties. We particularly like its nutty flavor and have been using it in many of our cakes and breads for over 15 years. Lots of alternative flour varieties are likewise enjoying a renaissance, such as almond flour (see page 197); polenta (see page 198); and chickpea, or gram, flour (see page 197). They taste naturally sweet, so your baking won't need as much additional sugar.

WHOLE-GRAIN FLOURS AND ANCIENT GRAIN VARIETIES, ON THE OTHER HAND, TASTE EARTHY, DIVERSE, AND NUTTY.

Natural sweeteners have additional baking properties. Dates (see page 198), for example, are highly aromatic. Dark brown sugar (see page 198) has a strong flavor of its own, reminiscent of caramel, while maple syrup (see page 198) or applesauce (see page 192) will ensure your cakes are really moist.

Why we are passionate about natural ingredients

As consumers, we have a choice about what we buy and eat. If we truly want a good future for our grandchildren, we should inevitably be opting for organic, regional, and seasonal produce. According to the *Washington Post*, of the over 900 pesticides used in agriculture in the US, only 25 are approved for use in organic farming, all of which have low toxicity. On the other hand, many of the pesticide substances used in conventional farming pose particular hazards for aquatic organisms, bees, other insects, and even humans. Official figures have revealed that conventional fruits and vegetables have up to 200 times the quantities of pesticides as organic products. And the residues from these toxins are found everywhere—particularly in water. Organic farms, on the other hand, are permitted to use only limited agents to combat pests. One of the central components of organic farming is to use sophisticated crop rotation systems to minimize weeds and to keep the soil fertile. In addition, small biotopes—uniform environments—are deliberately created by organic farmers to provide valuable habitats for wild plants, soil organisms, and other animals.

The best approach of course is to use organic products that are both seasonal and regional. Remember that when you buy produce in its natural season from your regional area, you are not only supporting local farms and businesses, but also doing something good for the natural world. It's not surprising that consuming locally farmed lettuce, tomatoes, or apples grown between spring and fall

(their natural growing season) achieves a better ecological balance than by importing fruits or vegetables from overseas during the same period.

Farmers who can sell their products at a local farmers' market don't need any intermediaries, which has many positive effects. The farmer can price goods more competitively, or at least consumers can be offered the price that would have been offered to the distributor. This in turn relieves the pressure to the farmer potentially caused by lower selling prices. The improved revenues from direct marketing can be invested by the farmer in better-quality farming techniques and in the products themselves. If the farmer sells seasonal products, these will have been freshly harvested, and because they don't need to be transported far, they can be picked at the optimum harvesting time. So fruits and vegetables can be left to ripen fully and develop all their vitamins and nutrients quite naturally. When these products arrive freshly harvested at your table, they are higher in quality and have a better flavor.

When products go into storage, things are a bit different. If Red Delicious apples are picked in October and stored in special conditions for several months, the energy consumption this requires can ultimately be higher than for imported apples. At around April, a point is reached where the energy balance tilts in favor of imported apples. But that doesn't change the fact that you can support local producers and thus retain more control over the food you buy. If you want to buy seasonal and regional fruits or vegetables, you should visit your local farmers' market or buy directly from the farmer. At farmers' markets, in particular, you will always find seasonal and regional products. In contrast to standard grocery stores, farmers' markets are always supplied by the producers themselves. If you are looking for exotic fruits, standard grocery stores usually supply these. Tropical fruits such as lemons and oranges provide variety in baking, especially in the winter months, and add a fresh note to a finished dish. For this reason, we don't avoid these fruits completely, but overall we have tried to minimize the use of exotic ingredients in this book.

Generally, we favor baking with regional and seasonal ingredients. With many products—especially eggs and dairy—we advocate using organic products for animal welfare reasons (see page 196). You can also get seasonal and regional products from conventional farming; however, since the standard rules on pesticide use and animal welfare are generally so lax, we often find that there is no alternative to buying organic.

We are by no means preaching that you should avoid all luxury foods and sugar. And we are not trying to force anyone to convert to veganism, vegetarianism, or an organic diet, nor do we advocate a paleo lifestyle or any other similar trend. We would just like to introduce you to baking with the most natural, original, and varied ingredients—exactly as they are found in nature. This also explains the title of our book: *Naturally Sweet Baking*. This book should inspire you to explore the multitude of natural flavors in these foods and also to bake with more unusual ingredients, such as parsnips (see page 155) or kidney beans (see page 168). You will be amazed what delicious baked goods you can conjure up!

Our recipes are marked with the following symbols to help you navigate the book:

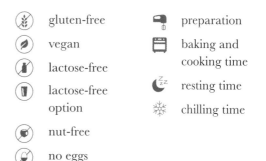

gluten-free		preparation	
vegan		baking and cooking time	
lactose-free		resting time	
lactose-free option		chilling time	
nut-free			
no eggs			

THE SCENT
OF LILAC

We know that spring has finally arrived when green
shoots start to pop up and anemones and violets
blossom in the woods. With the long-awaited start
of spring, we bake with the first rhubarb, early
strawberries, and delicate edible flowers, while lilac
blooms emit their beguilingly delightful scent.

APPLE TART

Walnut Frangipane, Maple Syrup, and Vanilla

Thanks to reliable natural storage methods, home-grown organic apples are available even in winter and spring, when they are still crisp and fresh, so our favorite fruit is always able to give this tart a harvest-fresh flavor. The crisp base is gluten-free, while the walnut cream rounds everything off perfectly.

☞ *MAKES 1 TART*

SHORTCRUST PASTRY

1 cup gluten-free
   rolled oats

2 tbsp flax seeds

$^1/_3$ cup buckwheat flour

$^1/_2$ cup cornstarch

2 tbsp dark brown sugar

pinch of salt

3 tbsp cold butter

$^1/_4$ cup cold buttermilk

FILLING

3oz (80g) walnuts

1 tsp ground cinnamon

$^1/_4$ cup maple syrup, plus
   1 tbsp for brushing

$^1/_4$ tsp vanilla extract

2 large eggs

1lb 5oz (600g) apples
   (4–5 apples)

2 tsp cold butter

Pulse the oats in a food processor to create a flour and set aside $^1/_4$ cup of the oat flour for the filling. Finely crush the flax seeds using a pestle and mortar. Combine $^1/_2$ cup of oat flour with the flax seeds, buckwheat flour, cornstarch, sugar, and salt in a bowl. Add the butter in little blobs and rub everything together with your fingers to form fine crumbs. Add the buttermilk and work quickly to combine. Avoid handling the dough too much; it should remain fairly lumpy. Wrap in plastic wrap and leave to rest for 20 minutes in the fridge.

To make the frangipane filling, grind the walnuts in a food processor to create a coarse flour. Place the remaining oat flour, cinnamon, maple syrup, vanilla extract, and eggs in a second bowl. Add the ground walnuts and stir until smoothly combined.

Preheat the oven to 350°F (180°C). Roll out the pastry on a sheet of parchment paper to create a large rectangle (roughly 11 × 12in/28 × 30cm) and place it on a baking sheet. Spread the frangipane on top, leaving a $^1/_2$in (1cm) border. Peel, quarter, and core the apples, then use a mandoline or knife to cut them into $^1/_8$in (3mm) thin slices. Arrange groups of five to six apple slices on the tart. Place the next group of slices at 90 degrees in a clockwise direction to the previous group and continue this way to make an attractive pattern. Dot little blobs of butter on top of the tart, fold up the edges, and press these in firmly.

Bake the tart in the center of the oven for 30–35 minutes. Brush the hot tart with maple syrup.

20 MINS   *30 MINS*   *30–35 MINS*

CARROT CAKE SWIRLS

Chickpea Flour, Vanilla, and Almonds

These little cakes are such a simple affair. At first glance, they seem unremarkable, but when eaten, the combination of carrots and high-protein chickpea flour gives them a really special zing. The natural sweetness of the applesauce and maple syrup rounds out the flavor.

☞ *MAKES 12 SMALL CAKES (DIAMETER 2¼IN/5.5CM)*

CAKE MIXTURE

2 large eggs

¼ tsp vanilla extract

5 tbsp maple syrup

½ cup mild olive oil, plus extra for greasing

½ cup applesauce (see page 192)

1 tsp ground cinnamon

1 cup chickpea flour, plus extra for dusting

⅓ cup ground almonds

⅓ cup cornstarch

2 tsp baking powder

pinch of salt

⅔ cup almond milk

5oz (150g) carrots, peeled and coarsely grated

ICING

1 batch cashew icing (see page 193; optional)

DECORATION

Forget-me-not flowers (optional)

Preheat the oven to 350°F (180°C). Whisk the eggs, vanilla extract, and maple syrup for a few minutes in a bowl, gradually adding the oil. Stir in the applesauce and cinnamon.

In a second bowl, combine the chickpea flour, almonds, cornstarch, baking powder, and salt. Add these dry ingredients to the egg mixture in stages, alternating with the milk. Stir everything gently, then fold the grated carrots into the cake mix.

Grease the cups of a muffin pan or mini bundt pan with oil and dust with flour. Transfer the mixture into the cups and bake for around 25 minutes, until risen and golden brown. When a toothpick inserted comes out clean, the little cakes are ready. Remove the cakes from the pan and leave to cool completely on a wire rack.

If icing the cakes, stir all the ingredients for the icing together. Cover the little cakes with the icing and, if using, decorate with forget-me-not flowers.

 🖨 *20 MINS*  *25 MINS*

RHUBARB TARTLETS

Crispy Almond Shortcrust and Coconut Yogurt

Rhubarb is one of the first indigenous "vegetables" that we particularly look forward to baking with after the long winter. In this recipe, we combine a perfectly balanced sweet and sour rhubarb-vanilla compote with coconut yogurt and almond shortcrust to conjure up spring on a plate.

☞ **MAKES 8 TARTLETS (DIAMETER 4IN/10CM)**

SHORTCRUST PASTRY

1¹/₃ cups spelt flour, plus extra for dusting

¹/₃ cup ground almonds

2 tbsp dark brown sugar

¹/₂ tsp baking powder

pinch of salt

¹/₄ cup mild olive oil, plus extra for greasing

baking beans, for blind baking

FILLING AND TOPPING

10oz (300g) rhubarb, peeled and sliced into 1¹/₂in (3cm) pieces

grated zest of ¹/₂ organic orange

¹/₄ cup maple syrup

1 vanilla bean, halved lengthwise and seeds removed

2¹/₄ cups coconut yogurt (see page 192)

Combine the flour, almonds, sugar, baking powder, and salt in a bowl. Add the oil and ¹/₄ cup water and work everything together quickly to form a dough. Avoid overhandling the dough; it should remain fairly lumpy. Shape into a ball, wrap in plastic wrap, and leave to rest for 20 minutes in the fridge.

Meanwhile, bring the rhubarb, orange zest, maple syrup, and vanilla bean and seeds to a boil in 3 tablespoons of water and simmer for 8–10 minutes, until soft. Leave the compote to cool.

Preheat the oven to 350°F (185°C). Grease 8 tartlet pans and dust with flour. Divide the pastry into 8 equal portions and roll each one out into a circle on a floured work surface. Line the tartlet pans with the pastry, press the edges slightly, and trim off any overhanging pastry. Prick the pastry bases several times with a fork and chill for 15 minutes. Line the bases with pieces of parchment paper cut to size, weigh each piece down with baking beans, and blind bake the pastry for 17–20 minutes in the center of the oven. Remove the baking beans and parchment paper, release the tartlets from their pans, and leave to cool. Fill with the coconut yogurt and top with the rhubarb compote.

Tip Decorate with a piece of vanilla bean on top of each tart to make these rhubarb tartlets a bit more exotic.

 35 MINS · 30 MINS · 17-20 MINS

Forget-me-not

Hollyhock

Lavender

Violets

Daisies

Gladioli

Elderflower

Sweet William

Horned violet

Rose

Dahlia

Blackberry flower

Borage

Thyme

Phlox

Lilac

Chamomile

Cornflower

Cosmos

Cherry blossom

Marigold

Apple Rose

French marigold

CARROT CAKE

Pumpkin Seeds, Apricots, and Honey-Yogurt Icing

☞ *MAKES 1 CAKE (DIAMETER 8IN/20CM)*

CAKE MIXTURE

2 large eggs

$^1/_2$ cup maple syrup

$^1/_4$ cup mild vegetable oil, plus extra for greasing

$^1/_4$ tsp black cardamom seeds

4 cloves

1 cup whole-grain spelt flour, plus extra for dusting

1 tsp ground cinnamon

pinch of grated nutmeg

2 tsp baking powder

pinch of salt

10oz (300g) carrots, peeled and finely grated

$^1/_3$ cup dried apricots, chopped

grated zest of $^1/_2$ organic orange

$^1/_3$ cup pumpkin seeds

ICING

5oz (150g) full-fat cream cheese

$^2/_3$ cup yogurt of choice

2 tbsp light honey

$^1/_2$ tsp vanilla extract

1 tbsp lemon juice

DECORATION

edible flowers and pumpkin seeds (optional)

Preheat the oven to 350°F (180°C). Beat the eggs and maple syrup in a bowl for several minutes with an electric mixer, gradually adding the oil. Finely grind the cardamom and cloves using a pestle and mortar. Combine the flour, spices, baking powder, and salt in a second bowl. Add to the egg and oil mixture and mix briefly. Fold the grated carrots, apricots, two-thirds of the orange zest, and the pumpkin seeds into the mixture.

Grease a springform pan (diameter 8in/20cm) with oil and dust with flour. Pour the cake mix into the pan, smooth the surface, and bake in the center of the oven for 35–40 minutes, until risen and golden brown. When a toothpick inserted comes out clean, the cake is ready. Carefully turn the warm cake out onto a wire rack and leave to cool completely.

For the icing, mix all the ingredients with most of the remaining orange zest and stir until smooth. Spread the mixture evenly over the cake. Sprinkle with the remaining orange zest and, if desired, decorate with edible flowers and some pumpkin seeds.

🕰 | 🖳 *25 MINS* 🗐 *35–40 MINS*

CHERRY BUNDT CAKE

Cacao Nibs and Vanilla

This bundt cake can be made all year round using frozen sour cherries. The cacao nibs are rich in magnesium and potassium and give the cake a strong chocolate flavor. In spring, you can decorate it with cherry blossoms in joyous anticipation of cherry season.

☞ *MAKES 1 BUNDT CAKE (DIAMETER 5¹/₂–6¹/₄IN/14–16CM)*

CAKE MIXTURE

3 tbsp softened butter, plus extra for greasing

¹/₂ cup dark brown sugar

3 large eggs

1 tsp vanilla extract

1¹/₃ cups whole-grain spelt flour

¹/₂ cup cornstarch

3 tsp baking powder

pinch of salt

¹/₃ cup milk of choice—we use almond milk

¹/₂ cup unsweetened sour cherries (jar or frozen)

¹/₄ cup cacao nibs

breadcrumbs for the pan

DECORATION

cherry and apple blossoms (as desired)

Preheat the oven to 350°F (180°C). In a bowl, cream the butter and sugar for 3–5 minutes with an electric mixer. Stir in the eggs one at a time and add the vanilla extract. In a second bowl, combine the flour, cornstarch, baking powder, and salt and stir the dry ingredients into the mixture a little at a time, stirring in some of the milk after each addition. Allow the thawed or preserved cherries to drain well, then carefully fold into the cake mix with the cacao nibs.

Grease a bundt pan with butter and sprinkle with breadcrumbs. Pour the cake mix into the pan and bake in the center of the oven for about 1 hour, until the cake has risen and is golden brown When a toothpick inserted comes out clean, the bundt cake is ready.

Leave to cool in the pan for about 10 minutes, then turn out onto a wire rack to cool completely. If you wish, decorate with cherry and apple blossoms.

Tip   *Instead of cacao nibs, you could also use chopped, high-quality dark chocolate with 70–85 percent cocoa content.*

🍴 *20 MINS*   🍳 *1 HR*

CHERRY HOT CROSS BUNS

With Nutmeg, Cinnamon, and Vanilla

These traditional Good Friday buns, which get their name from the characteristic cross made using a flour paste, are an extremely popular Easter treat. The secret ingredient in this particular recipe comes in the form of presoaked dried sour cherries.

☞ *MAKES 12 BUNS*

YEAST DOUGH

1 cup plus 1 tbsp milk of choice—we use almond milk

$1/3$ cup dark brown sugar

3 tsp active dry yeast

$1/2$ tsp vanilla extract

1 tsp ground cinnamon

pinch of grated nutmeg

pinch of salt

3 cups spelt flour, plus extra for dusting

4 tbsp softened butter

1 large egg

$1/2$ cup dried sour cherries (or cranberries or raisins)

$1/2$ cup orange juice

TOPPING

$1/3$ cup spelt flour

3 tbsp apricot jam (70 percent fruit content)

To make the yeast dough, heat the milk in a pan until lukewarm. Add the sugar, yeast, vanilla extract, cinnamon, nutmeg, and salt and stir well until the yeast has completely dissolved. Use the dough hook attachment on an electric mixer to combine the flour with the yeast mixture, butter, and egg for a couple of minutes in a bowl until you have a glossy and supple dough. The dough will be very soft and silky—exactly how it should be. Cover with a kitchen towel and leave to proof in a warm place for about 1 hour, until doubled in size. Meanwhile, soak the sour cherries in the orange juice. After about 1 hour, pour off the juice and leave to drain well.

Knead the dough thoroughly on a floured work surface and carefully work the sour cherries into the dough. Divide into 12 equal portions and shape into round buns. Place the buns, spaced a little apart, on two baking sheets lined with parchment paper. Cover with kitchen towels and leave to proof in a warm place for 30 minutes more.

To make the crosses, stir the flour into 2 tablespoons of water to form a smooth paste, transfer to a piping bag with a medium nozzle, and carefully pipe crosses onto the buns.

Preheat the oven to 350°F (185°C). Bake the hot cross buns in the center of the oven for about 16–19 minutes per sheet, until golden brown, then transfer to a wire rack and glaze with apricot jam while they are still hot. Serve while still warm; the buns go perfectly with some butter and jam.

🍴 20 MINS   🗄 32–38 MINS   🌙 90 MINS

DOUBLE CHOCOLATE MUFFINS

With Avocado Chocolate Mousse

These moist vegan chocolate muffins are given a special twist thanks to the espresso. The plant-based icing made from banana, avocado, and cocoa is a splendid addition and a healthier option than buttercream icing, while the violets add a sensual touch with their tantalizing scent.

☞ *MAKES 12 MUFFINS*

MUFFIN MIXTURE

2 tsp cider vinegar

1 cup almond milk

¹/₄ cup mild coconut oil

2 cups spelt flour

³/₄ cup dark brown sugar

6 tbsp cocoa powder

4 tsp baking powder

pinch of salt

2 tsp vanilla extract

¹/₄ cup cold espresso

FROSTING

2 ripe avocados

2 ripe bananas

3 tbsp maple syrup

¹/₄ cup mild coconut oil

8 tsp cocoa powder

1 tsp vanilla extract

DECORATION

24 violet flowers (optional)

Preheat the oven to 350°F (180°C). Whisk the cider vinegar and almond milk together in a bowl and set aside. Melt the coconut oil in a pan over low heat. Combine the flour, sugar, cocoa powder, baking powder, and salt in a large bowl. Add the almond milk mixture, melted coconut oil, vanilla extract, and espresso and stir briefly until combined.

Fill the cups of a muffin pan with 12 paper liners. Divide the mixture evenly between the liners and bake in the center of the oven for 18–22 minutes, until risen. When a toothpick inserted comes out clean, the muffins are ready. Remove from the pan and leave to cool on a wire rack.

To make the frosting, purée the avocado flesh, bananas, and remaining ingredients in a food processor until the frosting is glossy and silky-smooth. Chill in the fridge for 30 minutes, then transfer to a piping bag with a flower nozzle and pipe onto the muffins. If you wish, decorate with some violets.

🥄 *20 MINS*   🍞 *18–22 MINS*   ❄ *30 MINS*

ZUCCHINI CAKE

Elderflower, Pistachio, and Yogurt Icing

☞ MAKES 1 CAKE
(4¹/₂ × 10IN/
11 × 25CM)

CAKE MIXTURE

9 tbsp softened butter, plus
    extra for greasing

³/₄ cup dark brown sugar

3 large eggs

¹/₂ tsp vanilla extract

juice and grated zest of
    ¹/₂ organic lemon

1 cup pistachios

1¹/₃ cups spelt flour, plus extra
    for dusting

³/₄ cup whole-grain spelt flour

5 tsp baking powder

6 elderflower heads

14oz (400g) zucchini,
    finely grated

pinch of salt

ICING

¹/₂ tsp powdered sugar

¹/₂ tsp cornstarch

¹/₂ cup full-fat Greek yogurt

2 tbsp light honey

2 tsp lemon juice

DECORATION

2–3 elderflower heads

grated zest of ¹/₂ organic lemon

2 tbsp pistachios

1 tbsp pumpkin seeds

Preheat the oven to 350°F (180°C). Cream the butter and sugar in a bowl for 3–5 minutes, until light and fluffy. Stir in the eggs one at a time. Add the vanilla extract and the lemon juice and zest and mix. Finely grind the pistachios in a food processor or grinder. Combine the pistachios, both types of flour, and the baking powder. Add to the egg mixture and stir briefly. Shake the elderflower heads and strip off the flowers. Fold the zucchini, salt, and elderflowers into the cake mix.

Grease a loaf pan (4¹/₂ × 10in/11 × 25cm) with butter and dust with flour. Pour the cake mix into the pan and bake in the center of the oven for 35–40 minutes, until risen and golden brown. When a toothpick inserted comes out clean, the cake is ready. Leave to cool in the pan for about 10 minutes, then turn out onto a wire rack and leave to cool completely.

For the icing, stir the powdered sugar and cornstarch into the yogurt. Add the honey and lemon juice and combine until smooth. Spread the mixture evenly over the cake. Shake the elderflower heads and strip off the flowers. Decorate the cake with elderflowers, lemon zest, pistachios, and pumpkin seeds.

Tip   *This cake still tastes fantastic without the flowers outside of elderflower season. For a variation, instead of using ground pistachios, you can try ground almonds or hazelnuts.*

🔌 *25 MINS*   🍳 *35–40 MINS*

STRAWBERRY AND ALMOND MUFFINS

Almond Flour and Elderflowers

Spring meets summer in this recipe. The fragrant elderflowers give these muffins a unique flavor, and the combination of ripe strawberries with the delicate blossoms creates a real explosion of flavors. The gluten- and lactose-free almond flour helps to keep the muffins moist.

☞ *MAKES 10 MUFFINS*

MUFFIN MIXTURE

3 large eggs

$^1/_3$ cup dark brown sugar

$^1/_2$ tsp vanilla extract

$3^1/_2$ tbsp mild vegetable oil

$^3/_4$ cup buttermilk

1 cup almond flour

2 tsp baking powder

pinch of salt

3 elderflower heads

$3^1/_2$oz (100g) strawberries, hulled and chopped into small pieces

DECORATION

elderflowers and strawberry halves (as desired)

Preheat the oven to 350°F (180°C). Beat the eggs, sugar, and vanilla extract in a bowl for several minutes with an electric mixer until the mixture is pale. Add the oil and buttermilk. In a second bowl, combine the almond flour, baking powder, and salt. Add the dry ingredients in batches to the egg and buttermilk mixture.

Shake the elderflowers and strip off the flowers. Carefully fold the elderflowers and strawberry pieces into the muffin mixture. Fill the cups of a muffin pan with 10 paper liners. Divide the mixture evenly between the liners and bake the muffins in the center of the oven for 18–22 minutes, until risen and golden brown. When a toothpick inserted comes out clean, they are ready. Leave the muffins to cool on a wire rack. If you wish, decorate with the elderflowers and strawberries.

Tip *Outside of elderflower season, you can omit the flowers and just bake the muffins with strawberries.*

🔌 *15 MINS*   🍞 *18–22 MINS*

PEANUT BLONDIES

Chickpeas, Vanilla, and Dark Chocolate

Blondies are the pale sister of brownies. Our version is packed with peanut power, chickpea protein bombs, and dark chocolate—a superb flavor combination that is bound to boost your spirits. Moreover, if you make these in the food processor, they are very quick to prepare.

☞ *MAKES 9 BLONDIES*

BLONDIE MIX

1 cup chickpeas (from a jar, drained weight)

$1/4$ cup unsalted peanut butter

$1/4$ cup cashew butter

$1/4$ cup maple syrup

$1/2$ tsp vanilla extract

$1/2$ tsp baking powder

2oz (50g) dark chocolate, 70 percent cocoa content, chopped

coconut oil for greasing and teff flour or cornstarch for dusting

DECORATION

dark chocolate, 70 percent cocoa content, chopped (optional)

Preheat the oven to 350°F (180°C). Drain the chickpeas and wash thoroughly in cold water. Purée all the ingredients except the chocolate in a food processor until smooth, then add the chocolate and fold into the mix.

Grease a square baking pan (8–8$1/4$in/20–21cm) with coconut oil and dust with flour or cornstarch. Pour the blondie mixture into the pan, smooth the surface, and bake for about 25 minutes in the center of the oven, until pale golden in color. Leave to cool completely on a wire rack before cutting into pieces. If you wish, decorate with some chopped chocolate.

 Tip   *To make a vegan version, you could use vegan dark chocolate. If tightly sealed and stored in the fridge, the blondies will keep for 4–5 days.*

🥄 🍶 🍵 | 🔪 *10 MINS*   🗄 *25 MINS*

BUILDING BLOCKS: OAT MUFFINS

One Mix—Six Options

 MAKES 12 MUFFINS

①

THE BASIC MIX

3$\frac{1}{3}$ cups gluten-free rolled oats

1 tsp ground cinnamon

1 tsp baking powder

pinch of salt

1$\frac{3}{4}$ cups almond milk

1 tsp vanilla extract

$\frac{1}{2}$ cup maple syrup

oil and cornstarch for greasing and dusting

Combine the ingredients in a large bowl until mixed
well. Leave to swell for about 10 minutes. Preheat
the oven to 350°F (185°C). Grease the cups of a
muffin pan and dust with flour.

②

BLUEBERRY AND ALMOND

5oz (150g) blueberries

$\frac{2}{3}$ cup almonds, chopped

or

PEANUT BUTTER AND BANANA

9$\frac{3}{4}$oz (280g) bananas (about 2 bananas),
peeled and mashed

1 cup unsalted peanut butter

or

RASPBERRY AND CASHEW

5oz (150g) raspberries

$\frac{2}{3}$ cup cashews, chopped

or

APPLE AND CINNAMON

5oz (150g) apples, chopped (about 2 apples)

1 tsp ground cinnamon

or

CRANBERRY AND WALNUT

1 cup dried cranberries

grated zest of $\frac{1}{2}$ organic orange

$\frac{2}{3}$ cup walnuts, chopped

or

CARROT AND TURMERIC

$\frac{2}{3}$ cup carrot, finely grated

pinch of grated nutmeg

pinch of ground cloves

$\frac{1}{3}$ cup dried apricots, chopped

1 tsp grated turmeric

(3)

PREPARATION & BAKING

Add the chosen additional ingredients to the
muffin mixture and combine everything well.

Divide the mixture evenly between the
liners and bake in the center of the oven for
20–25 minutes, until the muffins are golden.
When a toothpick inserted comes out clean,
they are ready. Leave the muffins to cool on
a wire rack.

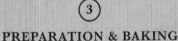

🥄 15 MINS   🍳 20–25 MINS   💤 10 MINS

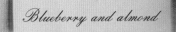

Blueberry and almond

Peanut butter and banana

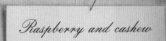

Raspberry and cashew

Apple and cinnamon

Cranberry and walnut

Carrot and turmeric

TEFF WAFFLES

Elderflower and Vanilla

When the first elderflower bushes begin to blossom in spring, we always make sure we take a basket and scissors on cycling excursions (see tip, below) because the window for harvesting these delicate, aromatic flowers is so brief. The white flower heads can be used for all sorts of recipes, both sweet and savory.

☞ *MAKES ABOUT*
8 WAFFLES
(3¹/₂ × 5¹/₂IN/
8.5 × 14CM)

BATTER

1 cup plus 1 tbsp milk of choice—we use almond milk

1¹/₄ tsp active dry yeast

¹/₃ cup dark brown sugar

2 large eggs

2 cups teff flour

³/₄ cup cornstarch

2 tsp baking powder

¹/₂ tsp vanilla extract

¹/₂ cup mild vegetable oil, plus extra for greasing

pinch of salt

6–8 elderflower heads

Heat the milk and ³/₄ cup water in a pan until lukewarm, then remove from the stove top. Dissolve the yeast and sugar in the lukewarm liquid.

Separate the eggs. In a bowl, combine the flour, cornstarch, and baking powder. Add the milk mixture, vanilla extract, and the egg yolks and stir until you have a smooth batter. Add the oil and stir it in. In a separate bowl, whisk the egg whites with the salt until stiff and carefully fold into the waffle mixture using a balloon whisk. Cover with a kitchen towel and leave to stand in a warm place for 20 minutes.

Shake the elderflower heads and strip off the flowers. Oil and preheat the waffle iron. For each waffle, put 2 tablespoons of the mix onto the iron, scatter with elderflowers, and cook until golden. Continue in this way until all the batter has been used. If you wish, serve the waffles with rhubarb compote (see page 22) and scatter raspberries on top.

Tip *It is best to pick elderflowers on a dry, sunny morning. Only then will the elderflowers be in full bloom and have their intense aroma. Always pick the flowers in open countryside to avoid potential pollution from traffic. The flowers wilt quickly, so you need to use them quickly. Don't rinse them because this will wash off the pollen, which provides the flavor. Once elderflower season is over, the waffles will still taste fantastic without their addition. You can vary this recipe by folding ¹/₃ cup of chopped almonds into the mix.*

🌾 🍶 | 📷 *15 MINS* 🍳 *12 MINS* 💤 *20 MINS*

BERRY ICE CREAM CAKE

Muesli Base and Berry Layers

This "nice cream" tart is ideal for hot days and offers a splendid alternative to heavy cream cakes. You won't need an oven for this recipe because this raw cake simply consists of a muesli base with berry ice cream layers. In early summer, you can decorate the cake with sweet lilac blossoms.

☞ *MAKES 1 CAKE (DIAMETER 8IN/20CM)*

BASE
1 cup unsweetened shredded coconut

1 cup almonds

3 tbsp mild coconut oil

$^2/_3$ cup dates

$^1/_2$ tsp vanilla extract

ICE CREAM LAYERS
7oz (200g) frozen blueberries

3 large bananas, about 1lb/450g

$1^1/_2$ tsp vanilla extract

7oz (200g) frozen blackberries

7oz (200g) frozen raspberries

DECORATION
5oz (150g) mixed frozen berries

lilac blossoms (optional)

Put all the ingredients for the base into a food processor and pulse until smooth. Transfer the mixture to a springform pan (diameter 8in/20cm) and press down to form an even base.

To make the blueberry layer, pulse the frozen blueberries, 1 banana (5oz/150g), and $^1/_2$ tsp of the vanilla extract in a food processor until you have a creamy ice mixture. Spread this over the muesli base and smooth the surface. Transfer to the freezer for 1–2 hours, until the bottom layer has set.

To make the blackberry layer, pulse the frozen blackberries, 1 banana (5oz/150g), and $^1/_2$ tsp of the vanilla extract in the food processor. Spread this mixture over the first layer and smooth the surface. Return to the freezer for another 1–2 hours, until the middle layer has set.

To make the raspberry layer, pulse the frozen raspberries, the remaining banana, and the rest of the vanilla extract in the food processor. Spread this mixture over the second layer and smooth the surface. Return to the freezer for a final 1–2 hours, until this top layer has set.

Let the cake defrost for 30–45 minutes before serving and decorate with frozen berries and lilac blossoms, as desired.

🔨 *30 MINS*   ❄ *3–6 HRS*   💤 *30–45 MINS*

FROM THE ORCHARD

The arrival of summer heralds the most perfect culinary paradise. Ripened sun-kissed berries hang from bushes, bringing joy to your plate, and you can make the most of the short season for stone fruit by indulging in exquisite cakes under clear blue skies.

RED CURRANT TEFF COOKIES

Hazelnuts and Dates

These red currant cookies are perfect for a quick break with a cup of tea. The gluten-free teff flour is rich in essential fatty acids, potassium, and phosphorous. Here, the flour combines beautifully with the red currants, dates, and hazelnuts to create a handy energy-boosting snack.

☞ *MAKES 12 COOKIES*

COOKIE DOUGH

$^2/_3$ cup hazelnuts

$^3/_4$ cup dried dates, finely chopped

$^2/_3$ cup teff flour

5 tbsp cornstarch

$^1/_2$ tsp baking powder

pinch of salt

7 tbsp cold butter

$^1/_2$ tsp vanilla extract

1 large egg

$3^1/_2$oz (100g) red currants

$^2/_3$ cup gluten-free rolled oats

Toast the hazelnuts in a dry pan over medium heat until pale brown and fragrant. Set aside and leave to cool. Place the dates in a saucepan with 2 tablespoons of water and bring to a boil, then simmer gently until soft. Purée and leave to cool.

Combine the teff flour, cornstarch, baking powder, and salt in a bowl. Add the butter in little blobs and rub everything together with your fingers to form fine crumbs. Add the date purée, vanilla extract, and egg and work everything quickly until combined. Avoid overhandling the dough; the texture should remain fairly lumpy. Coarsely chop the hazelnuts. Carefully work the red currants, oats, and hazelnuts into the cookie dough, trying not to squash the berries too much. Leave the dough to rest in the fridge for 30 minutes.

Preheat the oven to 350°F (180°C). Shape the cookie dough into 12 equal-sized balls. Place the balls some distance apart on two baking sheets lined with parchment paper and press them to flatten them slightly. Baking one sheet at a time, bake the cookies in the center of the oven for 12–15 minutes, until golden brown. Leave to cool—these very crumbly cookies become firmer as they cool. The cookies taste best fresh, but can also be stored in an airtight container in a cool place for 2–3 days.

Tip *Instead of using fresh red currants, these cookies can also be made with $^1/_2$ cup dried fruit, such as raisins, sour cherries, or cranberries. Soak the dried fruit beforehand in $^1/_4$ cup orange juice for 1–2 hours, then drain well before mixing into the cookie dough.*

🌾 | 🔨 *20 MINS*   🍳 *24–30 MINS*   ❄ *30 MINS*

SPRING SHEET CAKE

Raspberries, Fresh Currants, Strawberries, and Rhubarb

There is something here for everyone: tart rhubarb, sweet strawberries, the season's first raspberries, and fresh currants. Early summer offers only a brief window of opportunity for this exquisite combination of ingredients. This sheet cake is easy and quick to make, and the ingredients can be changed as you wish.

☞ *MAKES 1 CAKE*

CAKE MIX

18 tbsp soft butter

²/₃ cup light honey

5 large eggs

drop of vanilla extract

grated zest of 1 organic lemon

1³/₄ cups spelt flour

1 cup ground almonds

5 tsp baking powder

pinch of salt

¹/₂ cup milk of choice—we use
almond milk

FILLING

8oz (225g) raspberries

7oz (200g) strawberries, halved
and hulled

6oz (175g) fresh currants (white,
red, or black), stalks removed

4 sticks of rhubarb
(12in/30cm long)

1 tbsp dark brown sugar

Preheat the oven to 350°F (180°C). Cream the butter and honey in a bowl for 3–5 minutes. Stir in the eggs one at a time. Add the vanilla extract and lemon zest. In a second bowl, combine the flour, almonds, baking powder, and salt. Add the dry ingredients in batches to the butter mixture, alternating with the milk and mixing briefly.

Spread the mixture over a baking sheet lined with parchment paper. Arrange the raspberries, strawberries, currants, and rhubarb on separate quarters of the cake and sprinkle evenly with the sugar. Bake the cake in the center of the oven for 30–35 minutes, until risen and golden brown. When a toothpick inserted comes out clean, the cake is ready. Remove from the oven and leave to cool.

25 MINS   *30–35 MINS*

STRAWBERRY AND ALMOND CAKE

Almond Sponge Cake and Vanilla Cream

This cake has so many happy associations for us—from picking strawberries in our own garden to bicycle excursions to the pick-your-own farm. The light almond sponge cake is quick to make and is topped with a quark cream and plenty of fresh berries.

☞ **MAKES 1 CAKE (DIAMETER 10¹⁄₂IN/26CM)**

SPONGE CAKE

3 large eggs

¹⁄₂ cup dark brown sugar

pinch of salt

²⁄₃ cup ground almonds

¹⁄₄ cup cornstarch, plus extra for dusting

1 tsp baking powder

butter for greasing

TOPPING

9oz (250g) low-fat quark

1 tbsp maple syrup or honey

drop of vanilla extract

10oz (300g) strawberries, halved

5oz (150g) red currants or extra strawberries

daisies, to decorate (optional)

Preheat the oven to 375°F (190°C). Separate the eggs. In a bowl, beat the egg yolks with ¹⁄₄ cup of the sugar and 6 tablespoons of water using an electric mixer until thick and foamy. Whisk the egg whites separately with the salt until stiff, carefully pouring in the remaining sugar as you go. Combine the almonds, cornstarch, and baking powder. Carefully fold the whisked egg whites into the egg yolk mixture. Sift over the almond mixture and fold in quickly with a balloon whisk.

Grease a springform pan (diameter 10¹⁄₂in/26cm) with butter and dust with cornstarch. Pour the cake mix into the pan, smooth the surface, and bake in the center of the oven for 18–22 minutes, until risen and golden brown. When a toothpick inserted comes out clean, the cake is ready. Release from the pan and leave to cool on a wire rack.

To make the cream topping, stir the quark, maple syrup or honey, and vanilla extract together until smooth and spread evenly over the cake base. Scatter the fruit over the cake and, if you wish, decorate with daisies. Chill in the fridge for 30 minutes before serving.

⊛ | 🔨 *15 MINS*　🍳 *18–22 MINS*　❄ *30 MINS*

VICTORIA SPONGE CAKE

Raspberries and Rose Petals

In summer, we love indulging in leisurely picnics, and these occasions are never without a Victoria sponge cake. Our version uses spelt, raspberries, and rose water.

☞ **MAKES 1 CAKE (DIAMETER 8IN/20CM)**

CAKE MIX

11 tbsp softened butter, plus extra for greasing

$^1/_2$ cup dark brown sugar

$^1/_2$ tsp vanilla extract

3 large eggs

grated zest of $^1/_2$ organic orange

3 tbsp milk

1 cup whole-grain spelt flour, plus extra for dusting

2 tsp baking powder

pinch of salt

FILLING

$2^1/_2$ oz (75g) raspberries (fresh or frozen), plus raspberry jam

1 tsp dark brown sugar

20 drops rose water

$^1/_2$ cup whipping cream

$^1/_2$ tsp vanilla extract

1 tsp powdered sugar

1 tsp cornstarch

$^1/_2$ cup full-fat Greek yogurt

5oz (150g) raspberries

DECORATION

$3^1/_2$ oz (100g) raspberries

rose petals

Preheat the oven to 350°F (180°C). Cream the butter, sugar, and vanilla in a bowl for a few minutes using an electric mixer until the mixture is pale. Stir in the eggs one at a time. Add the orange zest and milk. In a second bowl, combine the flour, baking powder, and salt and add this in batches to the butter and egg mixture, stirring only briefly. Grease two springform pans (diameter 8in/20cm) with butter and dust with the flour. Divide the cake mix equally between the pans, smooth the surface, and bake in the center of the oven for 18–20 minutes, until the cakes have risen and are golden brown in color. When a toothpick inserted comes out clean, they are ready. Release from the pans and leave to cool on a wire rack for at least 30 minutes.

For the filling, bring the raspberries and sugar to a boil in a pan. Lower the heat and simmer for a couple of minutes, stirring occasionally until the liquid has reduced and resembles a thick jam in consistency. Leave the jam to cool, then stir in the rose water.

Whip the cream, vanilla, powdered sugar, and cornstarch until stiff, then fold in the yogurt. Place one of the cake halves on a cake platter and spread with jam. Cover with the whipped cream filling and most of the fresh raspberries. Place the second cake half on top. Decorate the cake with the extra raspberries and the rose petals. Chill in the fridge for 30–60 minutes before serving.

Tip *You could also try making this cake with strawberries!*

 20 MINS | **18–20 MINS** | **30–60 MINS** | **30 MINS**

APPLE WAFFLES

One Waffle—Lots of Toppings

Apple waffles with mineral-rich spelt flour are really easy to make and are a great alternative to traditional waffle recipes. Our version is vegan, and you can let your imagination run wild when it comes to the toppings. It won't be long before everyone in the family has decided on their favorite combo!

☞ *MAKES 10 HEART-SHAPED WAFFLES*

BATTER

2¼ cups plant-based milk— we use almond milk

3 tsp active dry yeast

½ cup maple syrup

4 cups spelt flour

2 tsp ground cinnamon

pinch of salt

⅔ cup mild vegetable oil, plus extra for greasing

14oz (400g) apples (about 3 apples), peeled and coarsely grated

toppings of choice, to serve (see tip, opposite)

Heat the milk in a pan until lukewarm, then remove from the stove top. Dissolve the yeast and maple syrup in the warmed milk. Combine the flour, cinnamon, and salt in a bowl. Add the milk mixture and the oil and whisk briefly using an electric mixer until you have a smooth batter. Cover with a kitchen towel and leave to proof in a warm place for 30 minutes to 1 hour.

Fold the grated apples into the batter. Oil and preheat the waffle iron. For each waffle, put 2 tablespoons of the mixture onto the iron and cook until golden. Continue in this way until all the batter has been used. Serve with fresh fruit, yogurt, or other toppings of your choice (see tip, below).

 Tip
Add one or more of the following toppings: blueberries, blackberries, fresh currants, raspberries, strawberries, apples, pears, damsons, grapes, bananas, frozen berries, (coconut) yogurt, fruit yogurt, fruit powder, maple syrup, honey, jam (70 percent fruit content), coulis made from frozen raspberries, almonds, cashews, hazelnuts, walnuts, pumpkin seeds, poppy seeds, popcorn, dark chocolate, cacao nibs, coconut chips, nut butters (such as peanut), applesauce, edible flowers, mint, and so on.

🖮 *15 MINS*   📟 *30 MINS*   💤 *30–60 MINS*

YOGURT CAKE

Einkorn, Gooseberries, and Red Currants

The yogurt in this recipe gives this cake a fresh, light texture and also adds moisture, while the protein-rich einkorn flour ensures a wonderful crispness. Combined with gooseberries and red currants, the result is a sweet and sour tang that is really addictive.

 MAKES 1 CAKE (DIAMETER 8IN/20CM)

CAKE MIX

2 large eggs

¹/₂ cup dark brown sugar

¹/₂ tsp vanilla extract

¹/₂ cup mild olive oil, plus extra for greasing

1 cup plus 1 tbsp yogurt of choice

1¹/₃ cups einkorn (or whole-grain spelt flour), plus extra for dusting

5 tsp baking powder

pinch of salt

5oz (150g) gooseberries, stalks removed

5oz (150g) fresh red currants

DECORATION

fresh red currants and gooseberries

dahlia flower petals (optional)

Preheat the oven to 350°F (180°C). In a bowl, cream the eggs, sugar, and vanilla extract with an electric mixer for a few minutes until the mixture is pale. Add the olive oil and yogurt and stir together. In a second bowl, combine the einkorn, baking powder, and salt and add this in batches to the egg and yogurt mixture. Stir briefly—just long enough to combine everything. Carefully fold the gooseberries and red currants into the cake mix.

Grease a springform pan (diameter 8in/20cm) and dust with some of the flour. Pour the cake mix into the pan, smooth the surface, and bake in the center of the oven for 35–40 minutes, until risen and golden brown. When a toothpick inserted comes out clean, the cake is ready. Release from the pan and leave to cool on a wire rack. For the decoration, arrange the berries together with the flower petals, if using, on the cake.

Tip   *Instead of gooseberries and red currants, berries such as raspberries and blackberries or fruit such as apricots and sour cherries also work well here.*

🔪 ⊗ | 🔪 *20 MINS*   ▤ *35–40 MINS*

"Čačak" damson

Mirabelle de
Nancy plum

"Graf Althans" greengage

Victoria plum

Large green greengage

Rheingold plum

Blue damson

Santa Rosa plum

Blue plum

BUCKWHEAT MUFFINS

Poppy Seeds and Plums

If you really want to savor the flavors of plum season, these muffins with crunchy oat crumble and poppy seeds are simply perfect. Poppy seeds are highly nutritious and rich in minerals, as well as cell-protecting vitamin E. The buckwheat flour adds a nutty element to the muffins.

☞ *MAKES 12 MUFFINS*

CRUMBLE TOPPING

2 tbsp cold butter

¼ cup gluten-free rolled oats

¼ cup buckwheat flour

3 tbsp dark brown sugar

½ tsp ground cinnamon

MUFFIN MIX

2 large eggs

½ cup dark brown sugar

½ tsp vanilla extract

½ cup mild olive oil

⅔ cup buttermilk

1 tbsp poppy seeds

1 cup buckwheat flour

1 cup cornstarch

2 tsp baking powder

pinch of salt

7oz (200g) yellow plums, damsons, or Mirabelle plums, halved, pitted, and chopped into small pieces

Preheat the oven to 350°F (180°C). To make the crumble, work all the ingredients together in a bowl until they resemble crumbs, then set aside.

For the muffin mix, beat the eggs, sugar, and vanilla extract for several minutes in a bowl using an electric mixer until the mixture is pale. Add the oil and buttermilk. In a second bowl, combine the poppy seeds, buckwheat flour, cornstarch, baking powder, and salt, then add this in batches to the egg and buttermilk mixture.

Carefully fold the fruit into the muffin mixture. Fill the cups of a muffin pan with 12 paper liners. Divide the mixture evenly between the liners and scatter over the crumble topping. Bake in the center of the oven for 18–22 minutes, until risen and golden brown. When a toothpick inserted comes out clean, they are ready. Leave the muffins to cool on a wire rack.

 15 MINS   *18–22 MINS*

VANILLA TARTLETS

Cherries, Peaches, Red Currants, and Pistachios

These exquisite and conveniently sized little tarts are ideal for a summer picnic or as a small snack between meals. The almond-milk custard filling is simple, quick to make, and also vegan. The pistachios add a nutty texture, which goes wonderfully with the summer fruit.

☞ **MAKES 8 TARTLETS (DIAMETER 8IN/10CM)**

SHORTCRUST PASTRY

1 1/3 cups spelt flour, plus extra for dusting

1/3 cup cornstarch

3 tbsp dark brown sugar

1/2 tsp baking powder

pinch of salt

2 tbsp mild vegetable oil, plus extra for greasing

baking beans, for blind baking

FILLING

1/4 cup cornstarch

1 3/4 cups almond milk

1/4 cup dark brown sugar

1 vanilla bean, halved and seeds removed

TOPPING

2 flat peaches, quartered and cut into very thin slices

24 sweet cherries

8 red currant stems

2 tbsp pistachios, chopped

Combine the flour, cornstarch, sugar, baking powder, and salt in a bowl. Add the oil and 2 tablespoons of cold water, then bring together quickly using your fingers. Avoid overhandling the dough; it should remain fairly lumpy. Shape it into a ball, wrap in plastic wrap, and rest for 20 minutes in the fridge.

Preheat the oven to 350°F (185°C). Grease the tartlet pans and dust with flour. Divide the pastry into 8 equal portions and roll each one out into a circle on a floured work surface. Line the tartlet pans with the pastry, press the edges slightly, and trim off any overhanging pastry. Prick the pastry bases several times with a fork and chill for 15 minutes. Cover the pastry with pieces of parchment paper cut to size, weigh each piece down with baking beans, and blind bake for 17–20 minutes in the center of the oven. Take the pans out of the oven and remove the baking beans and parchment paper. Release the tartlets from their pans and leave to cool completely on a wire rack.

To make the filling, stir the cornstarch into 1/4 cup of the almond milk until smooth. Put the remaining almond milk, sugar, and the vanilla bean and seeds into a pan and bring to a boil. Add the cornstarch paste to the pan, stirring constantly, bring to a boil again, and allow to simmer briefly until the custard thickens. Remove the vanilla bean, pour the custard into the tartlet crusts, and leave to cool for 30 minutes.

Arrange the peach slices, 3 cherries, and 1 strand of red currants on each tartlet. Scatter with the pistachios and chill for 10 minutes before serving.

🌿 🥄 ⊘ | 🔨 *20 MINS* | 📟 *17–20 MINS* | ❄ *45 MINS* | 💤 *30 MINS*

STONE FRUIT CRUMBLE

With Oat and Marzipan Topping

We love summer stone fruit! It doesn't matter if it's sour cherries, plums, or peaches. In high season, this sensational crumble is a fantastic opportunity to combine these vitamin-rich fruits. Energy-packed oat flakes mingle with marzipan and crunchy hazelnuts in the crumble layer.

☞ *MAKES 6–8*
   PORTIONS

FRUIT FILLING

2¼lb (1kg) mixed stone fruit (such as sour cherries, peaches, damsons, apricots, or plums), halved

1 apple, coarsely grated

½ tsp vanilla extract

½ cup unfiltered apple juice

CRUMBLE

⅓ cup hazelnuts, chopped

1¼ cups gluten-free rolled oats

1 cup whole-grain spelt flour

pinch of salt

½ cup vegan organic marzipan, cut into small cubes

¼ cup mild coconut oil

yogurt, to serve

Preheat the oven to 350°F (180°C). Transfer the stone fruit to a large casserole dish. Add the grated apple, vanilla extract, and apple juice and bake for 15 minutes. Stir everything once halfway through the cooking time.

Combine the hazelnuts, oats, flour, and salt in a bowl. Add the marzipan along with the coconut oil. Use your fingers to work everything into a crumble. Remove the casserole dish from the oven and scatter the crumble evenly over the fruit. Continue baking in the center of the oven for 20–25 minutes, until the crumble is golden brown. This dish is best served while still slightly warm. Serve with the yogurt of your choice.

🌿 🥜 🚫 | 🔪 *20 MINS* 🍳 *35–40 MINS*

CRUMBLE FLATBREADS

Gooseberries, Plums, and Greengages

At first glance, these crumble flatbreads can appear unremarkable, but eaten warm with an enticing combination of gooseberries, plums, and greengages, they are quite simply divine. Spelt crumble and vanilla add the finishing touches to this clever recipe, which is a big favorite of ours.

 MAKES 6–8 FLATBREADS

YEAST DOUGH

²/₃ cup milk of choice—we use almond milk

2 tsp dark brown sugar

1¹/₄ tsp active dry yeast

pinch of salt

2 cups spelt flour, plus extra for dusting

FRUIT TOPPING

1lb 2oz (500g) gooseberries, greengages, and plums, mixed

2 tbsp dark brown sugar

CRUMBLE

¹/₂ cup spelt flour

2 tbsp dark brown sugar

2 tbsp butter

drop of vanilla extract

To make the yeast dough, heat the milk until lukewarm. Add the sugar, yeast, and salt and stir well until the yeast has completely dissolved. Use the dough hook on an electric mixer to work the flour into the yeast mixture in a bowl for 2 minutes, until you have a glossy, supple dough. Cover with a kitchen towel and leave to proof in a warm place for about 1 hour, until doubled in volume.

Meanwhile, line a sheet with parchment paper. For the crumble, rub all the ingredients together in a bowl until they form rough crumbs and the vanilla extract is incorporated, and leave to chill in the fridge.

Knead the yeast dough once again on a floured work surface. Divide the dough into 6–8 portions and roll each one out to create a flatbread (roughly 5¹/₂ × 3¹/₄in/14 × 8cm), then place these on the baking sheet. Top the dough with a thick layer of fruit (cut surface upward), then sprinkle with the sugar and crumble. Cover the flatbreads and leave to proof for 30 minutes more.

Preheat the oven to 400°F (200°C). Bake the flatbreads in the center of the oven for 12–14 minutes. Serve warm.

Tip *For a vegan version, use the same quantity of mild coconut oil instead of the butter.*

20 MINS   *12–14 MINS*   *90 MINS*

APRICOT TART

Honey, Lavender, and Pine Nuts

This tart tastes like a summer greeting from Provence. Fresh apricots, honey, lavender, and pine nuts conjure up an enticing aroma that brings back memories of summer vacations in France.

☞ *MAKES 1 TART (DIAMETER 12IN/30CM)*

SHORTCRUST PASTRY

$1^1/_3$ cups whole-grain spelt flour (or whole-grain emmer flour), plus extra for dusting

2 tbsp dark brown sugar

pinch of salt

$^1/_3$ cup olive oil, plus extra for greasing

1 egg yolk

1 tbsp yogurt of your choice

baking beans, for blind baking

FRUIT FILLING

6–8 sprigs of lavender

2 tbsp pine nuts

1 tbsp mild olive oil

2 tbsp honey

$1^3/_4$lb (800g) apricots, halved and pitted

1 large egg

$^1/_2$ cup sour cream

ALSO

1 tbsp honey, for drizzling

Combine the flour, sugar, and salt in a bowl. Add the oil, egg yolk, and yogurt and bring together quickly to make the pastry dough. Avoid overhandling the dough; it should remain fairly lumpy. Shape it into a ball and roll out between two sheets of plastic wrap into a circle (diameter $14^1/_2$–15in/36–38cm). Remove the plastic wrap. Grease a tart pan, dust with flour, then line with the pastry. Press the edges down slightly and trim off any overhanging pastry. Prick the pastry base several times with a fork and transfer to the freezer for 30 minutes.

For the filling, shake the sprigs of lavender and strip off the flowers. Heat a large pan. Toast the pine nuts in the dry pan, remove, and set aside. Add the oil, honey, apricots, and lavender flowers and mix carefully. Cook over low heat for 3 minutes, then leave to cool.

Preheat the oven to 350°F (185°C). Line the tart pan with parchment paper, fill with baking beans, and blind bake for 10 minutes. Take the pastry pan out of the oven and remove the baking beans and parchment.

Whisk the egg and sour cream. Spread the egg mixture evenly over the base and top with the apricot mix. Bake the tart for 20–25 minutes in the center of the oven, then remove and leave to cool. Scatter with pine nuts and drizzle honey over the tart to serve.

Tip   *Of course, you can also bake this tart using peaches, figs, or grapes.*

 20 MINS   *30–35 MINS*   ❄ *30 MINS*

BUILDING BLOCKS: BUNDT CAKES

MAKES 1 BUNDT CAKE (DIAMETER 5½–6¼IN/14–16CM) OR 1 ROUND CAKE (DIAMETER 8IN/20CM)

① THE BASIC INGREDIENTS	② TO SWEETEN	③ FAT	④ FLOUR
3 large eggs	½ cup dark brown sugar *or* 5 tbsp honey *or* ⅓ cup maple syrup	6 tbsp butter *or* 6 tbsp mild coconut oil, warmed *or* ⅓ cup mild vegetable oil	1⅓ cups spelt flour *or* 1 cup teff flour + ¾ cup cornstarch *or* 1⅓ cups einkorn flour *or* 1⅓ cups emmer flour
Preheat the oven to 350°F (180°C). Grease a baking pan (bundt pan diameter 6–7in/14–16cm or springform pan diameter 8in/20cm) and dust with flour. Whisk the eggs in a bowl.	Add the sweetener and whisk well.	Gradually add the fat.	Combine the flour with 2 tsp baking powder and a pinch of salt and add in batches to the cake mix with ⅓ cup of your chosen milk.

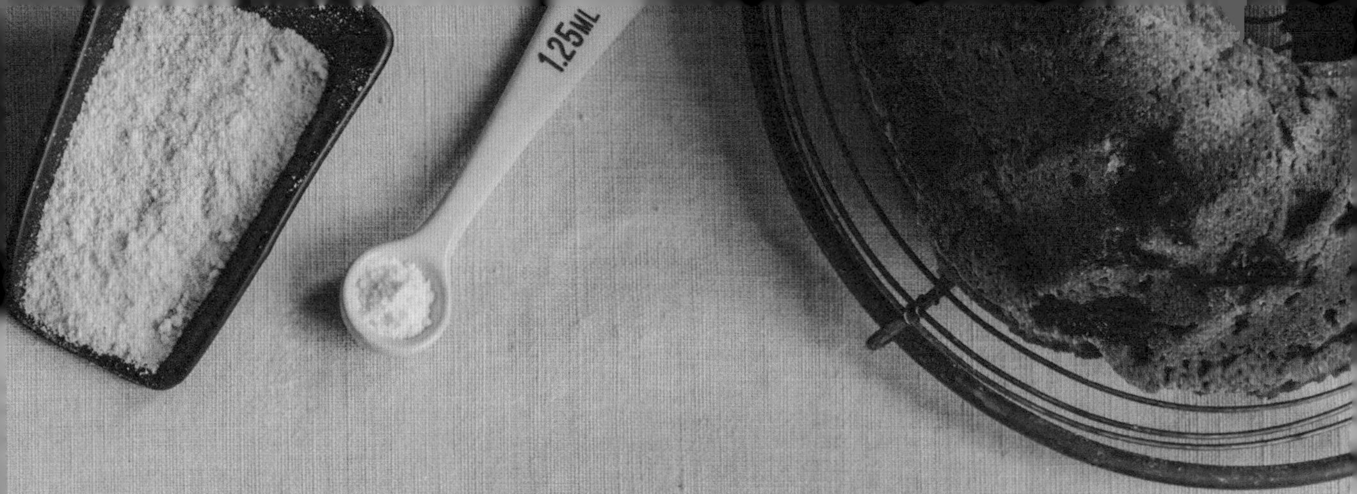

⑤ SOME FRUIT

5oz (150g) frozen
cherries, defrosted, or
fresh cherries, pit
removed

or

5oz (150g) berries

or

5oz (150g) chopped
apple (about 2 apples)

Fold the fruit into the
cake mixture.

⑥ ADDED FLAVOR

1 tsp ground cinnamon

or

$1/2$ tsp vanilla extract

or

pinch of ground black
cardamom seeds

Add the flavor and mix
together well.

⑦ A BIT OF CRUNCH

2 tbsp almonds,
chopped

or

2 tbsp hazelnuts,
chopped

or

2 tbsp walnuts, chopped

or

1 tbsp dark chocolate,
chopped

Fold the nuts or
chocolate into the
cake mix and pour
the mixture into your
pan. Bake the bundt
cake for 50–55 minutes,
or a round cake for
30–35 minutes. Insert a
toothpick to test if done.

🍽 | 🔨 *20 MINS*   🍞 *30–35 OR 50–55 MINS*

CHERRY TART

Crunchy Almond Crumble and Vanilla Custard

☞ **MAKES 1 TART (DIAMETER 12IN/30CM)**

SHORTCRUST PASTRY

1 cup teff flour, plus extra for dusting

$^1/_2$ cup cornstarch

$^1/_4$ cup dark brown sugar

pinch of salt

9 tbsp butter, plus extra for greasing

1 large egg

baking beans, for blind baking

FRUIT FILLING

3oz (85g) dried dates, finely chopped

2oz (60g) cornstarch

drop of vanilla extract

grated zest and juice of $^1/_2$ organic orange

2lb (900g) frozen sour cherries, defrosted

1 vanilla bean, halved lengthwise and seeds removed

CRUMBLE

$^1/_3$ cup gluten-free rolled oats

1 tbsp teff flour

$^1/_2$ tsp ground cinnamon

2 tbsp dark brown sugar

2 tbsp mild coconut oil

$^1/_3$ cup sliced almonds

For the pastry, combine the flour, cornstarch, sugar, and salt in a bowl. Add the butter and rub together with your fingers to form fine crumbs. Add the egg and 2 tablespoons of water and work quickly to create the pastry dough. Avoid overhandling the dough; it should remain fairly lumpy. Wrap in plastic wrap and chill in the fridge for 30 minutes.

To make the filling, put the dates in a pan with $^1/_3$ cup water, bring to a boil, then simmer gently until soft. Purée and leave to cool. Stir the cornstarch and vanilla extract into the orange juice until smoothly combined. Bring the puréed dates back to a boil, adding the orange zest, cherries, and vanilla bean and seeds, and simmer gently for 5 minutes. Stir the custard mixture into the hot cherries, bring briefly to a boil, and cook for 1 minute. Remove the vanilla bean and leave the cherry mixture to cool.

To make the crumble, combine the oats, flour, cinnamon, and sugar. Work in the coconut oil, rubbing everything together with your fingers until it forms a crumbly consistency. Fold in the almonds, then chill the crumble.

Preheat the oven to 350°F (180°C). Grease the tart pan and dust with flour. Roll out the dough on a floured work surface into a large circle (diameter $14^1/_2$–15in/36–38cm). Transfer into the tart pan, press the edges down slightly, and trim off any overhanging pastry. Prick the pastry base several times with a fork and chill for 15 minutes, then line with parchment paper, fill with baking beans, and blind bake in the center of the oven for 20 minutes. Take the pastry pan out of the oven and remove the baking beans and parchment.

Spread the cherry mixture evenly over the pastry and top with the crumble. Bake the tart for 25 minutes, then increase the oven temperature to 400°F (200°C) and bake for 5 minutes more, until golden brown. Leave to cool on a wire rack, then remove from the pan.

🕸 🥛 | 🔨 *35 MINS* 📟 *50 MINS* ❄ *45 MINS*

RASPBERRY AND BLACKBERRY COBBLER

With an Oat and Corn Crust

If you like pies, you will love this cobbler. The term "cobbler" is indeed linked to the job description cobbler and comes from the phrase "to cobble something together." Here, baked sweet fruit is topped with a crisp, golden polenta crust, which gives it a distinctive crunch.

☞ *MAKES 4–6 PORTIONS*

FRUIT FILLING

1 apple, coarsely grated

10oz (300g) raspberries (fresh or frozen)

10oz (300g) blackberries (fresh or frozen)

1 tsp cornstarch

2 tsp lemon juice

1 tsp ground cinnamon

THE COBBLER MIX

$^2/_3$ cup gluten-free rolled oats

$^1/_2$ cup cornstarch

$^1/_4$ cup polenta

$^1/_3$ cup whole cane sugar

1 tsp baking powder

pinch of salt

5 tbsp cold butter

5 tbsp almond milk

yogurt, to serve

Preheat the oven to 350°F (180°C). Put the grated apple, raspberries, blackberries, cornstarch, lemon juice, and cinnamon in a pan and bring to a boil. Lower the heat and allow the fruit to simmer very briefly. Transfer the fruit to a casserole dish (about 7 × 10$^1/_2$in/18 × 26cm).

Grind the oats in a food processor to make a flour. Combine the ground oats, cornstarch, polenta, sugar, baking powder, and salt in a bowl. Add the butter in little blobs and rub everything together with your fingers to create a crumble. Add the almond milk and work this briefly into the mixture until combined. Divide the cobbler mix into 8 equal-sized balls, press each one slightly flat, and arrange them on top of the stewed fruit. Bake the cobbler in the center of the oven for 35–40 minutes, until golden brown. This dish tastes best slightly warm and served with a yogurt of your choice.

Tip   *For a vegan version, use the same quantity of mild coconut oil instead of the butter. This recipe also tastes fabulous with other fruits, such as fresh currants, strawberries, or stone fruits.*

20 MINS   35–40 MINS

OAT WAFFLES

Yogurt and Honey

Oats are rich in vitamins B1 and B6. Using a food processor, you can make your own oat flour in no time, which can be used to bake fantastic, moist waffles. These waffles are delicious for breakfast, afternoon snacks—or at any time, to be honest.

☞ *MAKES ABOUT 4 WAFFLES (3½ × 5½IN / 8.5 × 14CM)*

BATTER

2 large eggs

¼ cup honey (or maple syrup)

⅔ cup milk of choice—we use almond milk

½ cup plain yogurt or coconut yogurt

1¾ cups gluten-free rolled oats

1 tsp ground cinnamon

2 tsp baking powder

pinch of salt

oil for the waffle iron

fresh fruit, yogurt, or other toppings (see tip, page 60), to serve

Beat the eggs, honey, milk, and yogurt in a bowl using an electric mixer. Grind the oats in a food processor to make a flour. In a second bowl, combine the ground oats, cinnamon, baking powder, and salt. Add this to the milk mixture and stir everything gently.

Oil and preheat the waffle iron. For each waffle, put 2 tablespoons of batter onto the iron and cook until golden. Continue in this way until all the batter has been used. Serve with fresh fruit, yogurt, or the topping of your choice (see tip, page 60).

10 MINS   *12 MINS*

BLUEBERRY PANCAKES

Light Batter and Buttermilk

These pancakes are very light and fluffy thanks to the buttermilk and whisked egg whites, while the blueberries add a sweet, fruity element. This recipe is bound to become one of your all-time classic favorites for weekend breakfasts.

☞ *MAKES 8–10 PANCAKES*

BATTER

3 large eggs

$^1/_2$ cup buttermilk

$^3/_4$ cup spelt, emmer, or einkorn flour, or $^2/_3$ cup gluten-free flour mix

2 tsp baking powder

pinch of salt

some oil for the pan

7oz (200g) blueberries

DECORATION

blueberries and phlox flowers (optional)

Separate the eggs. Beat the egg yolks with the buttermilk in a bowl using an electric mixer. In a second bowl, combine your chosen flour with the baking powder. Add this to the buttermilk mixture and stir everything gently to form a thick batter. Whisk the egg whites with the salt until stiff, and carefully fold this into the batter using a balloon whisk.

Heat some oil in a large pan and add 1–2 tablespoons of batter for each pancake, scatter over a few blueberries, and cook for 2–3 minutes, until golden brown and firm underneath. Flip the pancakes and continue cooking until the other side is also nice and golden. Continue in this way until all the batter has been used, keeping the cooked pancakes warm as you work. Scatter the blueberries over the pancakes and decorate with phlox flowers, if using.

Tip   *These pancakes taste best drizzled with some maple syrup. Instead of blueberries, the pancakes also taste fabulous with bananas, chopped apples, or other berries.*

 🎙 *12 MINS*   🍞 *8–10 MINS*

Elderberries

Wild
strawberries

Cranberries

Black currants

Red raspberries

Yellow
raspberries

White currants

Blueberries

Blackberries

Red currants

Wild blueberries

Gooseberries

Strawberries

Lingonberries

RICOTTA CHEESECAKE

Cookie Base, Banana, and Raspberry Coulis

The world-famous New York cheesecake was invented in 1872 by William Lawrence from Chester, New York. With just a couple of simple tweaks, you can bake a slightly lighter, less sweet version. Ripe bananas, ricotta cheese, and sour cream ensure a creamy consistency.

☞ **MAKES 1 CAKE (DIAMETER 8IN/20CM)**

BASE

5oz (150g) spelt or whole-wheat cookies

5 tbsp butter, melted

CHEESECAKE FILLING

1 large ripe banana, mashed

1lb 2oz (500g) ricotta cheese

1 cup sour cream

5 tbsp light honey

grated zest of ¹/₂ organic lemon

1 tbsp cornstarch

3 large eggs

RASPBERRY COULIS

5oz (150g) frozen raspberries, defrosted

¹/₄ tsp vanilla extract

2 tbsp light honey

DECORATION

3¹/₂oz (100g) raspberries

2oz (50g) red currants (optional)

Put the cookies in a freezer bag and gently crush with a rolling pin to form crumbs. Combine the cookie crumbs and butter in a bowl. Line a springform pan (diameter 8in/20cm) with parchment paper, pour the crumbs into the pan, carefully press them flat to make the base, and chill briefly in the fridge.

Preheat the oven to 300°F (150°C). Beat together the mashed banana, ricotta cheese, sour cream, honey, lemon zest, and cornstarch in a bowl, then stir in the eggs one at a time. Fill an oven-safe dish with water and place this on the bottom of the oven. Pour the cheesecake mixture into the pan and bake in the center of the oven for 55–60 minutes, until the filling has set. When you shake the pan gently, you should still see a bit of a "jelly wobble." Leave the cheesecake to cool completely.

Remove the cheesecake from the pan. To make the coulis, purée the frozen raspberries, vanilla extract, and honey and drizzle over the cheesecake. Decorate the cheesecake with the raspberries and, if using, the red currants.

 🍴 | 🔌 *20 MINS* 📟 *55–60 MINS*

BLACKBERRY BUNDT CAKE

Cardamom and Blueberry Icing

In summer, we love collecting wild blackberries while out cycling, then once back at home, we use the fruit to try out new recipes. One of these is this bundt cake made using chickpea flour. The flour is very rich in protein, and its excellent baking properties help to make the cake wonderfully moist.

☞ **MAKES 1 BUNDT CAKE (DIAMETER 5¹/₂–6¹/₄IN/14–16CM)**

CAKE MIX

3 large eggs

drop of vanilla extract

¹/₂ cup maple syrup

¹/₂ cup mild vegetable oil

¹/₂ tsp black cardamom seeds

³/₄ cup chickpea flour

1 cup teff flour

3 tsp baking powder

pinch of salt

²/₃ cup almond milk

3¹/₂oz (100g) blackberries (fresh or frozen)

coconut oil and polenta, for greasing and dusting

ICING

1 batch cashew icing (see page 193)

2 tsp blueberry fruit powder

DECORATION

2¹/₂oz (75g) blackberries

Preheat the oven to 350°F (180°C). Beat the eggs, vanilla extract, and maple syrup in a bowl for several minutes with an electric mixer, gradually adding the oil. Finely grind the cardamom using a pestle and mortar. In a second bowl, combine both types of flour, cardamom, baking powder, and salt. Add this to the egg mixture, alternating with the almond milk until everything is well mixed. Carefully fold the blackberries into the cake mixture.

Grease a bundt pan with coconut oil and dust with polenta. Pour the cake mixture into your pan and bake in the center of the oven for 1 hour, until risen and golden brown. When a toothpick inserted comes out clean, the bundt cake is ready. Leave to cool in the pan for about 10 minutes, then turn out onto a wire rack and leave to cool completely.

Color the cashew icing with the blueberry fruit powder and ice the bundt cake. Wash and pat dry the blackberries, and decorate the cake.

 Tip *Instead of blackberries, you could also try making this bundt cake using the same quantity of blueberries. To make sure the decorative blackberries stay in place, you can secure them using toothpicks that have been cut in half.*

 *20 MINS* *1 HR*

BLACK CURRANT SPIRALS

Whole-grain Emmer, Vanilla, and Honey

Of all the berries, we think black currants are the unsung heroes—their exceptional flavor is absolutely unique. They also provide plenty of vitamin C and have anti-inflammatory properties. Here, the black currants are given center stage in these crisp yet soft spirals.

☛ *MAKES 12 SPIRALS*

YEAST DOUGH

1¼ cups milk of choice—
   we use almond milk

1 tsp vanilla extract

⅓ cup dark brown sugar

2¼ tsp active dry yeast

pinch of salt

4 cups whole-grain
   emmer flour, plus extra
   for dusting

6 tbsp softened butter,
   plus extra for greasing

FILLING

10oz (300g) black currants,
   stalks removed (or red
   currants)

¼ cup light honey

To make the yeast dough, heat the milk and vanilla extract in a pan until lukewarm. Add the sugar, yeast, and salt and stir well until the yeast has completely dissolved. Use the dough hook attachment on an electric mixer to combine the flour with the milk mixture and the butter in a bowl for a couple of minutes, until you have a glossy and supple dough. Cover with a kitchen towel and leave to proof in a warm place for 1 hour, until doubled in volume.

Grease the cups of a muffin pan and dust with flour. Knead the dough thoroughly on a floured work surface and roll it out into a rectangle (about 11 × 15in/28 × 38cm). Scatter the dough with black currants and drizzle over the honey. Roll up the rectangle from the long side and slice the roll into 12 sections. Place each piece into a muffin pan cup. Cover with a kitchen towel and leave to proof in a warm place for 30 minutes more.

Preheat the oven to 425°F (220°C). Bake the spirals in the center of the oven for 8–10 minutes, then remove and leave to cool on a wire rack.

20 MINS   *8–10 MINS*   *90 MINS*

LATE SUMMER BERRY GATEAU

Light Sponge Cake, Citrus Notes, and a Medley of Berries

At the height of summer, the different berry bushes in the garden virtually explode with fruit. The perfect dish for this time is our berry gateau with its light sponge cake, low-fat curd cheese, and colorful berries. If you like berries, you're going to be thrilled with this recipe.

☞ *MAKES 1 CAKE (DIAMETER 8IN/20CM)*

SPONGE CAKE

5 large eggs

1/2 cup dark brown sugar

grated zest of 1/2 organic orange

pinch of salt

1/2 cup ground almonds

1/2 cup cornstarch

2 tsp baking powder

butter and cornstarch for greasing and dusting

FILLING

1 1/4 cups low-fat quark

6oz (175g) full-fat cream cheese

1 tsp powdered sugar

1 tsp cornstarch

3 tbsp maple syrup

1/2 tsp vanilla extract

grated zest of 1/2 organic lemon

9oz (250g) mixed berries

DECORATION

5oz (150g) mixed berries and blackberry flowers (optional)

Preheat the oven to 375°F (190°C). Separate the eggs. In a bowl, beat the egg yolks and 6 tablespoons of the sugar with 10 tablespoons of water and the orange zest using an electric mixer until thick and foamy. Whisk the egg whites with the salt until stiff, carefully pouring in the remaining sugar as you go. Gently fold the whisked egg whites into the yolk and sugar mixture. In another bowl, combine the almonds, cornstarch, and baking powder and sift this over the egg mixture. Fold in briefly using a balloon whisk.

Grease just the bases of two springform pans (diameter 8in/20cm) with butter and dust with cornstarch. Divide the cake mix equally between the pans, smooth the surface, and bake in the center of the oven for 18–22 minutes, until the cakes have risen and are golden brown in color. When a toothpick inserted comes out clean, they are ready. Release the cakes from the pans and leave to cool completely on a wire rack.

To make the filling, stir together all the ingredients except the berries. Place one of the cakes on a cake platter. Spread two-thirds of the cream over this base. Cover with berries, then put the second cake on top and spread over the remaining cream. Decorate the cake with berries and blackberry flowers, if using. Chill in the fridge for 30–60 minutes before serving.

🌾 | 🔨 *25 MINS*　📟 *18–22 MINS*　❄ *30–60 MINS*

SPELT WAFFLES

Belgium-style

These wholesome waffles with fresh berries are perfect for breakfast or for a weekend brunch. Our version of these Belgium-style yeasted waffles uses nutritious spelt flour and substitutes dark brown sugar for the traditional pearl sugar.

☞ *MAKES ABOUT 8 WAFFLES (3½ × 5½IN/8.5 × 14CM)*

BATTER

9 tbsp butter, plus extra for greasing

1 cup plus 1 tbsp milk of choice—we use almond milk

½ tsp vanilla extract

1½ tsp active dry yeast

⅓ cup dark brown sugar

2 large eggs

1¾ cups whole-grain spelt flour

1¾ cups spelt flour

1 tsp ground cinnamon

1 tsp baking powder

pinch of salt

selection of fresh fruit, to serve

DECORATION

blackberry flowers (optional)

Melt the butter in a pan over medium heat. Add the milk, vanilla extract, and ¾ cup of water; heat until lukewarm; and remove from the stove top. Dissolve the yeast and sugar in the lukewarm liquid.

Separate the eggs. In a bowl, combine both types of flour, cinnamon, and baking powder. Add the milk mixture and egg yolks and use an electric mixer to create a smooth batter. In a separate bowl, whisk the egg whites with the salt until stiff and carefully fold into the waffle mixture using a balloon whisk. Cover with a kitchen towel and leave to stand in a warm place for 20 minutes.

Grease and preheat the waffle iron. For each waffle, put 2 tablespoons of the batter onto the iron and cook until golden. Continue in this way until all the batter has been used. Fresh fruit is the perfect accompaniment with these waffles. If you wish, decorate with blackberry flowers.

 Tip *These waffles can also be cooked ahead of time and frozen. Heat them up individually in the toaster—they will taste as good as when freshly cooked.*

🖫 *10 MINS*   ▦ *24 MINS*   ☾ᶻᶻ *20 MINS*

BLUEBERRY GALETTE

Delicate Yogurt Shortcrust and Hints of Citrus

In August, we love to pick homegrown blueberries from pick-your-own farms that grow this superfood. Once you are back home, making this warm tart can be your reward. These super berries are also rich in vitamins, minerals, and other important micronutrients.

☞ *MAKES 1 GALETTE*

SHORTCRUST BASE

1¹⁄₃ cups whole-grain einkorn flour, plus extra for dusting

¹⁄₂ cup polenta

3 tbsp dark brown sugar

pinch of salt

6 tbsp cold butter

¹⁄₄ cup yogurt of choice

FRUIT TOPPING

1lb (450g) blueberries

2 tsp cornstarch

2 tbsp dark brown sugar

2–3 drops vanilla extract

grated zest and 1 tbsp juice of ¹⁄₂ organic lemon

ALSO

2 tbsp milk of choice

1 tsp dark brown sugar

yogurt or vanilla ice cream, to serve

Preheat the oven to 400°F (200°C). Combine the flour and polenta with the sugar and salt in a bowl. Add the butter in little blobs and rub the ingredients with your fingers until combined. Avoid overhandling the dough; the texture should remain fairly lumpy. Stir the yogurt into ¹⁄₄ cup water, add to the bowl, and work quickly into the other ingredients. Wrap in plastic wrap and chill in the fridge for 20 minutes.

Meanwhile, mix the blueberries with the other topping ingredients.

Dust a piece of parchment paper with the flour and roll out the shortcrust into a large disc (diameter about 11in/28cm). Use the parchment paper to transfer the pastry onto a baking sheet. Spread the filling out in the center, leaving a 1¹⁄₂in (3cm) border around the edges. Fold up the edges of the pastry over the filling and press gently into place. Brush the edge with milk and sprinkle with the sugar. Bake the galette in the center of the oven for 25–30 minutes, until golden brown. The galette tastes best served warm with yogurt or a scoop of vanilla ice cream.

Tip *Of course, this recipe also works with frozen blueberries, too. Just defrost the berries and let them drain beforehand.*

BLACKBERRY SWISS ROLL

Almond Sponge Cake and Vanilla-Quark Cream

Swiss roll is an absolute classic and hugely popular with us. We use almond flour here because it retains plenty of moisture, which gives the sponge cake an excellent texture. A light quark cream together with jam, fresh berries, and flowers add the finishing touches to this violet summer dream.

☛ *MAKES 1 SWISS ROLL (8–10 PIECES)*

SPONGE CAKE

5 large eggs

$^1/_2$ cup dark brown sugar, plus extra for coating

2–3 drops vanilla extract

pinch of salt

$^1/_2$ cup almond flour

$^1/_2$ cup cornstarch

FILLING

2–3 drops vanilla extract

2 tbsp maple syrup

$1^3/_4$ cups low-fat quark

$^1/_4$ cup whipping cream

1 tsp cornstarch

1 tsp powdered sugar

$^1/_2$ cup blackberry jam, 70 percent fruit content

9oz (250g) blackberries

DECORATION

$2^1/_2$oz (75g) blackberries and blueberries, mixed

purple basil leaves and sweet William flowers (optional)

Preheat the oven to 375°F (190°C). Separate the eggs. In a bowl, beat the egg yolks and $^1/_3$ cup of the sugar with 10 tablespoons of water and the vanilla extract using an electric mixer, until thick and foamy. Whisk the egg whites with the salt until stiff, carefully pouring in the remaining sugar as you go. Combine the almond flour and cornstarch in another bowl. Carefully fold the whisked egg whites into the egg yolk mixture with a balloon whisk. Sift over the flour mixture and quickly fold this in, too. Line a baking sheet with parchment paper. Spread the sponge cake mixture over the sheet to make a roughly 13 × 13in (34 × 34cm) square. Bake in the center of the oven for 9–11 minutes, until the sponge cake has risen and is golden yellow.

Place a clean kitchen towel that is larger than your cake on the work surface and sprinkle evenly with sugar. Turn the cooked cake out onto a board and carefully peel off the parchment paper, then transfer the cake to the prepared kitchen towel so that the smooth cake base is in contact with the towel. Trim the cake all around to straighten the edges. Quickly roll up the cake with the kitchen towel while the cake is still warm and leave to cool like this.

Stir the vanilla extract and maple syrup into the quark until smooth. Beat the cream with the cornstarch and powdered sugar until it holds its shape, and fold this into the quark. Gently unroll the sponge cake and spread with a layer of jam followed by the cream, leaving a $^1/_2$in (1cm) border free at the edges. Scatter over the blackberries. Roll up the cake once again, using the kitchen towel to help you, and slide the cake onto a plate with the seam facing down.

Decorate the Swiss roll with berries and, if you wish, scatter with basil leaves and flowers. Chill for 30 minutes before serving.

🥄 | 🖾 *25 MINS*　　📟 *9–11 MINS*　　❄ *30 MINS*

BLACKBERRY CHEESECAKES

Whole-wheat Cookie Base and Blackberry Coconut Cream

Ripe blackberries are super juicy and full of vitamins, not to mention low in calories, and they have a sweet and sour flavor. We've captured their enticing forest flavor in this light, airy cheesecake. The fruity quark and coconut cream topping sits on a crunchy whole-wheat cookie base, which doesn't require any baking.

☞ *MAKES 4 CHEESECAKES (DIAMETER 3¼IN/8CM)*

BASES

3oz (80g) whole-wheat cookies

3 tbsp butter, melted

CREAMY TOPPING

1³/₄ cups low-fat quark

3oz (80g) frozen blackberries, defrosted, or fresh blackberries

¹/₄ cup light honey

2–3 drops vanilla extract

grated zest and 2 tbsp juice from 1 organic lime

¹/₃ cup coconut milk

1 tsp cornstarch

1 tsp powdered sugar

DECORATION

2¹/₂oz (75g) blackberries

blackberry flowers (optional)

Put the whole-wheat cookies into a freezer bag and crush gently with a rolling pin to form crumbs. Combine the cookie crumbs and butter in a bowl. Place four food presentation rings (diameter 3¹/₄in/8cm) on a flat dish lined with parchment paper. Put a quarter of the cookie crumb mix into each ring, carefully pressing each base flat, then transfer to the fridge.

For the creamy topping, use an electric mixer on the highest setting to purée the quark, blackberries, honey, vanilla extract, and lime zest and juice in a high-sided container. Gently heat the coconut milk in a pan, add the cornstarch and powdered sugar, and stir. Add spoonfuls of the blackberry mixture to the coconut milk mixture until the temperatures are roughly equal, then stir both mixtures together. Pour the cream into the preprepared molds and chill in the fridge for 2 hours, until the topping has set.

To serve, release the cheesecakes from the ring molds, arrange on a plate, and decorate with blackberries and, if you wish, blackberry flowers.

Tip   *You could also prepare these cheesecakes in glasses or small bowls.*

🥄 *20 MINS*   ❄ *2 HRS*

BLUEBERRY NAKED CAKE

Hazelnut Sponge Cake, Coconut Cream, and Blueberry Jam

☞ *MAKES 1 CAKE*
  (DIAMETER
  8IN/20CM)

JAM

5oz (150g) frozen or fresh
  blueberries

2 tbsp dark brown sugar

CAKE MIX

³/₄ cup hazelnuts

4 large eggs

¹/₂ cup dark brown sugar

¹/₃ cup mild vegetable oil, plus
  extra for greasing

¹/₂ cup applesauce
  (see page 192)

2–3 drops vanilla extract

1 cup whole-grain emmer flour
  or whole-grain spelt, plus
  extra for dusting

3 tsp baking powder

pinch of salt

¹/₃ cup almond milk

FILLING

double batch of coconut cream
  (see page 193)

7oz (200g) blueberries

DECORATION

edible flowers: horned violets,
  borage, purple basil (optional)

Bring the blueberries and sugar to a boil in a pan. Lower the heat and simmer the berries for a couple of minutes, until the liquid has reduced and the consistency resembles thick jam. Stir occasionally during cooking, then leave the jam to cool.

Toast the hazelnuts in a dry pan until pale brown. Leave to cool completely before grinding finely in a food processor.

Preheat the oven to 350°F (185°C). Beat the eggs and sugar in a bowl for several minutes with an electric mixer, until the mixture is a pale cream color. Add the oil, applesauce, and vanilla extract and stir. In a second bowl, combine the ground hazelnuts, flour, baking powder, and salt, then add this in batches to the egg mixture, alternating with the milk. Take care not to stir too much once combined.

Grease two springform pans (diameter 8in/20cm) with oil and dust with the flour. Divide the cake mixture equally between the pans, smooth the surface, and bake in the center of the oven for 20–25 minutes, until risen and golden. When a toothpick inserted comes out clean, the cakes are ready. Remove the cakes from the pans and leave to cool completely on a wire rack.

Briefly chill the coconut cream for the filling. Place one of the cakes on a cake platter. Fold the jam into the coconut cream using a spatula, taking care not to blend them completely, and spread half the mixture over the cake. Spread half the blueberries over the cream, place the second cake on top, and cover with the remaining blueberry and coconut cream. Scatter over the remaining blueberries and decorate the cake as desired with edible flowers. Chill in the fridge for 30–60 minutes before serving.

🗲 25 MINS   📟 20–25 MINS   ❄ 30–60 MINS

BERRY PIZZA

Ricotta Cheese, Light Honey, and Pine Nuts

This fantastic sweet pizza made using a crunchy spelt dough is not only utterly delicious, the baking process is really fun, too! Spread with a bit of ricotta cheese, then feel free to finish it off as you please with a selection of healthy berries. A bit of honey adds a subtle sweetness, and mint gives it a fresh zing.

☞ *MAKES 1 PIZZA (DIAMETER 11IN/28CM)*

YEAST DOUGH

¹/₃ cup milk of choice—we use almond milk

1 tbsp dark brown sugar

1³/₄ tsp active dry yeast

pinch of salt

1¹/₂ cups spelt flour, plus extra for dusting

1¹/₂ tbsp mild olive oil

FRUIT TOPPING

10oz (300g) mixed berries (blueberries, raspberries, black currants, red currants, white currants)

¹/₃ cup ricotta cheese

2–3 tbsp light honey

2 tbsp pine nuts

a few mint leaves

To make the yeast dough, heat the milk in a pan until lukewarm. Add the sugar, yeast, and salt and stir everything well. Put the flour and oil into a bowl. Add the milk mixture and use the dough hook attachment on an electric mixer to process everything for a few minutes, until you have a glossy, supple dough. Cover with a kitchen towel and leave to proof in a warm place for 1 hour, until doubled in volume.

Meanwhile, set aside a few of the berries for decorating. Line a sheet with parchment paper and preheat the oven to 400°F (200°C).

Knead the yeast dough once again on a floured work surface and roll it out to create a circle (diameter 11in/28cm), shaping the edges to come up slightly higher. Lay the dough on a baking sheet, spread ricotta evenly over the surface, and top with a densely packed layer of berries. Drizzle with honey and scatter over the pine nuts. Bake the pizza in the center of the oven for 20–23 minutes. Remove from the oven and scatter over the mint leaves and reserved berries.

20 MINS ｜ 20–23 MINS ｜ 1 HR

ELDERBERRY GATEAU

Dark Chocolate, Cardamom, and Coconut Cream

☞ *MAKES 1 CAKE (DIAMETER 8IN/20CM)*

COMPOTE

1 tsp cornstarch

¹/₄ tsp black cardamom seeds

5oz (150g) elderberries, stalks removed

¹/₄ cup light honey

CAKE MIX

3¹/₂oz (100g) dark chocolate, 70 percent cocoa content

4 large eggs

²/₃ cup light honey

¹/₂ cup mild coconut oil, plus extra for greasing

2–3 drops vanilla extract

1 cup whole-grain einkorn flour, plus extra for dusting

¹/₂ cup ground almonds

3 tsp baking powder

pinch of salt

¹/₃ cup milk of choice—we use almond milk

FILLING

1 batch coconut cream (see page 193)

DECORATION

2¹/₂oz (75g) blackberries, edible flowers, purple basil leaves (optional)

To make the compote, stir the cornstarch into 3 tablespoons of water. Finely grind the cardamom seeds using a pestle and mortar. Bring the elderberries, cardamom, and honey to a boil in a pan and simmer rapidly for 1–2 minutes. Add the cornstarch mixture, stirring constantly, and bring to a boil briefly until the compote has thickened slightly. Set aside and leave to cool.

Preheat the oven to 350°F (180°C). Coarsely chop the chocolate and melt over a double boiler. Beat the eggs and honey for several minutes in a bowl with an electric mixer until the mixture is a pale cream color. Gradually add the coconut oil and vanilla extract. In a second bowl, combine the flour, almonds, baking powder, and salt, then add this in batches to the egg mixture, alternating with the milk. Take care not to stir too much once combined. Stir in the melted chocolate.

Grease two springform pans (diameter 8in/20cm) with coconut oil and dust with flour. Divide the cake mixture equally between the pans, smooth the surface, and bake in the center of the oven for 20–25 minutes, until risen and golden brown. When a toothpick inserted comes out clean, the cakes are ready. Leave to cool on a wire rack. Briefly chill the coconut cream.

Once the cakes are cool, place one of them on a cake platter and spread with half the coconut cream. Cover this with about two-thirds of the compote and place the second cake on top. Finally, add the remaining coconut cream followed by the remaining compote. Decorate the gateau as desired with blackberries, edible flowers, and basil. Chill for 30–60 minutes before serving.

Tip *If you can't get ahold of elderberries, you can make the gateau with frozen sour cherries or cranberries.*

 🔪 *25 MINS*   ▤ *20–25 MINS*   ❄ *30–60 MINS*

A RICH HARVEST

As the dahlias come into bloom, we head slowly into fall. The last of the blackberries gladden our hearts, while plump, rosy-cheeked apples; colorful pears; golden quinces; and sweet, late-season plums are just waiting to be harvested and complemented with wonderful flavors.

"SAVE A BANANA" PANCAKES

Whole-grain Spelt Flour and Walnuts

Of all fruit, overripe bananas are the most likely to end up in the trash. This pancake recipe is great for exploiting the sweetness of fully ripe bananas and avoiding waste. You can also use overripe bananas in our moist banana bread (see page 166).

 MAKES 8 PANCAKES

BATTER

1 large ripe banana, mashed

1 large egg

$^3/_4$ cup milk of choice—we use almond milk

2 tbsp mild coconut oil, warmed, plus extra for cooking

1–2 drops vanilla extract

$^3/_4$ cup whole-grain spelt flour

$^1/_2$ tsp ground cinnamon

$^1/_2$ tsp baking powder

$^1/_2$ cup walnuts, coarsely chopped

Combine the mashed banana with the egg, milk, coconut oil, and vanilla extract using an electric mixer. In a second bowl, combine the flour, cinnamon, and baking powder. Add this to the banana mixture and stir gently to create a thick, smooth batter. Fold the walnuts into the batter.

Heat some coconut oil in a pan and add $1^1/_2$–2 tablespoons of batter for each pancake. Cook for 2–3 minutes, until the underside is golden and firm, then flip the pancakes and continue cooking until the other side is also nice and golden. Continue in this way until all the batter has been used. Keep the cooked pancakes warm as you work.

Tip   *The pancakes taste best warm, drizzled with some maple syrup. Fresh fruit such as figs or berries also go with these pancakes beautifully.*

 10 MINS   *10 MINS*

HAZELNUT BUNDT CAKE

Maple Syrup and Beet Icing

Marbled bundt cakes are a regular feature at our house. This version uses hazelnuts that have been roasted and ground, giving the cake a very intense nutty flavor. With its colorful beet icing and berry topping, this classic recipe has become a favorite cake for birthdays!

☞ *MAKES 1 BUNDT CAKE (DIAMETER 8¹⁄₂IN/22CM)*

CAKE MIX

1¹⁄₂ cups hazelnuts

18 tbsp softened butter, plus extra for greasing

²⁄₃ cup maple syrup

5 large eggs

2–3 drops vanilla extract

1¹⁄₂ cups spelt flour, plus extra for dusting

5 tsp baking powder

pinch of salt

²⁄₃ cup milk of choice—we use almond milk

1 tbsp rum

ICING

1 batch cashew icing (see page 193)

2 tsp beet powder

DECORATION

2oz (50g) blackberries

1oz (30g) blueberries

Toast the hazelnuts in a dry pan until pale brown, then leave to cool completely. Finely grind 1¹⁄₃ cups of the hazelnuts in a food processor, chop the remaining hazelnuts, and set both aside.

Preheat the oven to 350°F (180°C). Cream the butter in a bowl with an electric mixer for several minutes until pale. Stir in the maple syrup, the eggs one at a time, and the vanilla extract. In a second bowl, combine the flour, ground and chopped hazelnuts, baking powder, and salt. Add this in batches to the egg mixture, alternating with the milk and rum and mixing gently.

Grease a bundt pan (diameter 8¹⁄₂in/22cm) with butter and dust with the flour. Pour the cake mixture into the pan and bake in the center of the oven for 50 minutes to 1 hour, until risen and golden brown. When a toothpick inserted comes out clean, the bundt cake is ready. Leave the bundt cake to cool in the pan for about 10 minutes, then turn it out onto a wire rack and leave to cool completely.

Color the cashew icing with the beet powder and use to ice the bundt cake. Decorate the cake with the blackberries and blueberries.

Tip *To make sure the blackberries stay in place, you can secure them using toothpicks that have been cut in half.*

🖐 *20 MINS*　　🍴 *50–60 MINS*

PLUM CAKE

Cinnamon and Vanilla Crumble

This sheet cake brings back unforgettable childhood memories of the plum harvest in our grandmother's garden. Baking this classic together was an annual ritual. Our updated version is crammed with plums and is less sweet, while the cinnamon gives it a sophisticated twist.

☞ *MAKES 1 SHEET CAKE*

YEAST DOUGH

³/₄ cup milk of choice—we use almond milk

2 tbsp dark brown sugar

3 tsp active dry yeast

pinch of salt

2 cups plus 2 tbsp spelt flour, plus extra for dusting

4 tbsp softened butter

FRUIT TOPPING

3lb 3oz (1.5kg) plums

1 tbsp dark brown sugar

2 tsp ground cinnamon

CRUMBLE

³/₄ cup spelt flour

3 tbsp dark brown sugar

2–3 drops vanilla extract

4 tbsp cold butter

DECORATION

phlox flowers (optional)

To make the yeast dough, heat the milk in a pan until lukewarm. Add the sugar, yeast, and salt and stir well. Use the dough hook on an electric mixer to combine the flour, yeast mixture, and butter in a bowl for a couple of minutes, until you have a glossy, supple dough. Cover with a kitchen towel and leave the dough to proof in a warm place for 1 hour, until doubled in volume.

Meanwhile, for the crumble, rub all the ingredients together in a bowl until you have coarse crumbs. Leave to chill in the fridge.

Knead the yeast dough once again on a floured work surface and roll it out to the size of your sheet. Transfer onto a sheet lined with parchment paper. Cover the dough with a closely packed layer of plums (cut surface facing up) and scatter with the sugar, ground cinnamon, and the crumble. Cover the cake and leave to proof once more for 30 minutes.

Preheat the oven to 350°F (180°C). Bake the plum cake in the center of the oven for 35–40 minutes, then remove and leave to cool. If you wish, decorate with phlox flowers.

Tip *For a vegan version, you can replace the butter with the same quantity of coconut oil and use a plant-based milk. This cake also tastes great with other varieties of plums or with chopped apples.*

Ⓘ Ⓘ Ⓘ | 🕐 *30 MINS*   🍞 *35–40 MINS*   💤 *90 MINS*

BLUEBERRY "FRANZBRÖTCHEN"

Cardamom, Vanilla, and Dates

"Franzbrötchen," a traditional speciality in Hamburg, Germany, are made using puff pastry or a yeast-leavened dough and are often served with coffee. Traditionally, the filling is packed with fat and sugar; our version is baked using a juicy blueberry filling and has a hint of cardamom.

☞ *MAKES 12 BUNS*

YEAST DOUGH

1¼ cups milk of choice—we use almond milk

½ tsp black cardamom seeds

⅓ cup dark brown sugar

1 tsp ground cinnamon

2¼ tsp active dry yeast

pinch of salt

4 cups spelt flour, plus extra for dusting

5 tbsp softened butter

FILLING

2½oz (75g) dried dates, chopped

9oz (250g) frozen blueberries (ideally wild)

1 tsp ground cinnamon

1–2 drops vanilla extract

grated zest of ½ organic lemon

To make the yeast dough, heat the milk in a pan until lukewarm. Grind the cardamom seeds using a pestle and mortar. Add the cardamom, sugar, cinnamon, yeast, and salt to the milk and stir well until the yeast has completely dissolved. Use the dough hook attachment on an electric mixer to combine the flour with the milk mixture and the butter in a bowl for a couple of minutes, until you have a glossy and supple dough. Cover with a kitchen towel and leave to proof in a warm place for 1 hour, until doubled in volume.

Meanwhile, for the filling, place the dates in a pan with 2 tablespoons of water, bring them to a boil, and simmer until soft. Purée and leave to cool. Bring the blueberries to a boil in another pan and simmer down until the juice has almost completely evaporated. Stir in the date purée, cinnamon, vanilla extract, and lemon zest and leave to cool.

Knead the dough thoroughly on a floured work surface and carefully roll it out into a rectangle (about 12 × 15½in/30 × 40cm). Cover the dough evenly with the filling. Roll up the rectangle from the long side and slice the roll into 12 sections. Place the swirls onto two sheets lined with parchment paper, cover with kitchen towels, and leave to proof in a warm place for 30 minutes more.

Preheat the oven to 425°F (220°C). Bake each sheet of swirls in the center of the oven for 8–10 minutes.

 Tip *For a vegan version, you can use the same quantity of mild coconut oil instead of the butter and a plant-based milk instead of cow's milk.*

🔧 *15–20 MINS*   🍞 *16–20 MINS*   💤 *90 MINS*

BUCKWHEAT BUNDT CAKE

Cranberries and Dark Chocolate

In the Celle region in Lower Saxony, Germany, buckwheat cake with lingonberries is a real classic, but cranberries are a good substitute. Here, we have reinterpreted the traditional recipe in bundt cake form. The cranberries keep the buckwheat sponge cake moist, a chocolate glaze adds the finishing touch, and the whole cake is crowned with fresh figs.

☞ *MAKES 1 BUNDT CAKE (DIAMETER 8¹/₂IN/22CM)*

CAKE MIX

5 large eggs

³/₄ cup dark brown sugar

1 cup plus 1 tbsp mild vegetable oil, plus extra for greasing

2–3 drops vanilla extract

1 cup buckwheat flour, plus extra for dusting

¹/₂ cup cornstarch

1¹/₃ cups ground hazelnuts

5 tsp baking powder

pinch of salt

²/₃ cup almond milk

2oz (50g) dark chocolate, 70 percent cocoa content, coarsely chopped

7oz (200g) frozen cranberries, thawed

ALSO

1oz (30g) dark chocolate, 70 percent cocoa content, coarsely chopped

3 fresh figs, quartered

Preheat the oven to 350°F (180°C). Beat the eggs and sugar in a bowl for several minutes with an electric mixer, gradually adding the oil and vanilla extract as you go. In a second bowl, combine the flour, cornstarch, hazelnuts, baking powder, and salt. Add this in batches to the egg mixture, alternating with the milk and mixing everything gently. Add the chocolate to the mixture, carefully folding it in along with the cranberries.

Grease a bundt pan (diameter 8¹/₂in/22cm) with oil and dust with the flour. Pour the cake mix into the pan and bake in the center of the oven for 50–55 minutes, until risen and golden brown. When a toothpick inserted comes out clean, the bundt cake is ready. Leave to cool in the pan for about 10 minutes, then turn out onto a wire rack and leave to cool completely.

To make the icing, melt the chocolate over a double boiler. Decorate the bundt cake with the chocolate glaze and arrange the figs on top.

 Tip

To make a lactose-free version, you can use vegan dark chocolate. Instead of cranberries, you could also use sour cherries. To make sure the decorative figs stay in place, you can secure them using toothpicks that have been cut in half.

🖤 🎂 | 🔌 *20 MINS* 📟 *50–55 MINS*

"Celler Dickstiel"

Red-fleshed

Red Boskoop

Idared

"Wellant"

"Delbarestivale"

Ananas Reinette

Elstar

Glockenapfel

"Roter Imperiale"

Pinova

APPLE CAKE

Ginger, Cloves, and Cinnamon

Apple cake is one of our absolute favorites. It brings back reassuring childhood memories of Sunday afternoon tea with granny in the fall, making the most of the apple harvest from the garden. Our version is made with einkorn flour, maple syrup, warming spices, and lots of apples.

☞ MAKES 1 CAKE
(DIAMETER
10½IN/26CM)

CAKE MIX

3 large eggs

pinch of salt

5 tbsp softened butter, plus
   extra for greasing

²/₃ cup maple syrup, or
   ³/₄ cup dark brown sugar

seeds from 1 vanilla bean

2 cups einkorn flour, plus extra
   for dusting

pinch of ground ginger

pinch of ground cloves

1 tsp ground cinnamon, plus
   extra for sprinkling

2 tsp baking powder

²/₃ cup almond milk

1 tbsp rum

ALSO

1lb 10oz (750g) apples (about
   4 apples), peeled, quartered,
   and cored

2 tbsp apricot jam, 70 percent
   fruit content

Preheat the oven to 350°F (185°C). Separate the eggs. Beat the egg whites and salt in a bowl with an electric mixer until stiff. In another bowl, cream the butter for several minutes until pale. Add the maple syrup and egg yolks, stir everything together, and add the vanilla seeds. Combine the flour, spices, and baking powder and gradually add to the mix, alternating with the almond milk and rum and mixing everything gently. Finally, gently fold in the egg whites with a balloon whisk. Make parallel incisions in each apple quarter.

Grease a springform pan (diameter 10½in/26cm) and dust with some of the flour. Pour the mixture into the pan, smooth the surface, and arrange the apple quarters on top. Bake the cake in the center of the oven for 40–45 minutes, until risen and golden brown. When a toothpick inserted comes out clean, the cake is ready. Leave the cake to cool in the pan for about 10 minutes, then turn out onto a wire rack and leave to cool completely.

Heat the apricot jam in a pan over low heat and use this to brush the cake while it is still warm. Finally, sprinkle with a little cinnamon and leave to cool on a wire rack.

 20 MINS   🍳 40–45 MINS

APPLE CRUMBLE MUFFINS

Cinnamon, Ginger, and Marzipan Crumble

In this recipe, we combine two popular classics—apple crumble and muffins—with nutritious spelt flour and marzipan crumble. A hint of ground ginger lends a touch of sophistication. These muffins taste absolutely fantastic eaten while still slightly warm.

☞ *MAKES 12 MUFFINS*

CRUMBLE TOPPING

²⁄₃ cup spelt flour

1 tsp dark brown sugar

2 tbsp cold butter

2 tbsp organic marzipan

MUFFIN MIX

2 large eggs

²⁄₃ cup buttermilk

¹⁄₃ cup mild vegetable oil

2–3 drops vanilla extract

¹⁄₂ cup dark brown sugar

1¹⁄₂ cups spelt flour

2 tsp baking powder

¹⁄₂ tsp ground cinnamon

pinch of ground ginger

pinch of salt

7oz (200g) apples (about
2 apples), peeled, quartered,
cored, and chopped into
small pieces

Preheat the oven to 350°F (180°C). To make the crumble, rub all the ingredients together in a bowl to form crumbs, then set aside.

For the muffin mix, whisk the eggs, buttermilk, oil, and vanilla extract in a bowl. In a second bowl, combine the sugar, flour, baking powder, cinnamon, ground ginger, and salt. Add the wet ingredients to the dry and beat briefly using an electric mixer, until the mixture is smooth and silky.

Fill the cups of a muffin pan with 12 paper liners. Carefully fold the chopped apples into the muffin mix and divide the mixture evenly between the liners. Partially bake the muffins in the center of the oven for 8 minutes, remove from the oven, and scatter over the crumble topping. Continue cooking the muffins for another 12–14 minutes, until risen and golden brown. When a toothpick inserted comes out clean, they are ready. Leave the muffins to cool on a wire rack.

🔨 *25 MINS*   🍳 *20–22 MINS*

BLACKBERRY AND APPLE PIE

Crunchy Spelt Pastry and Cinnamon

Blackberries and apples are like Ginger Rogers and Fred Astaire: they complement each other perfectly and are a guaranteed hit. The apples are slightly more dominant in terms of taste, while the sweet and tangy blackberries add flavor and give the pie filling its deep red color.

☞ **MAKES 1 PIE (DIAMETER 9¹⁄₂IN/24CM)**

SHORTCRUST PASTRY

2¹⁄₄ cups spelt flour, plus extra for dusting

pinch of salt

11 tbsp cold butter, plus extra for greasing

2 tbsp maple syrup

1 large egg

2 tbsp milk of choice—we use almond milk

FILLING

2¹⁄₄lb (1kg) apples (about 6 apples), peeled

9oz (250g) blackberries

¹⁄₂ cup dark brown sugar

1–2 drops vanilla extract

1 tsp ground cinnamon

grated zest and 1 tbsp juice from 1 organic lemon

ALSO

1 egg yolk

1 tbsp milk of choice—we use almond milk

1 tbsp dark brown sugar

yogurt, to serve

Combine the flour and salt in a bowl. Add the butter in little blobs and rub everything with your fingers to form fine crumbs. Add the maple syrup, egg, and milk and work in quickly. Avoid overhandling the pastry; it should remain fairly lumpy. If it looks too dry, add a bit more milk. Wrap the pastry in plastic wrap and chill in the fridge for 30 minutes.

Coarsely grate one apple. Quarter the others, remove the cores, and slice each quarter in half lengthwise. Combine the chopped and grated apple with the blackberries, sugar, vanilla extract, cinnamon, and lemon juice and zest.

Preheat the oven to 350°F (180°C). Grease a tart pan (diameter 9¹⁄₂in/24cm) and dust with the flour. Roll out half the pastry on a floured work surface into a circle (diameter 12–13in/30–34cm). Transfer into the tart pan, press the edges down slightly, and trim off any overhanging pastry. Pour the filling into the pastry crust and brush the pastry rim with a bit of water. Roll out the remaining pastry, slice into 1³⁄₄–2in (4–5cm) wide strips, and place these in a lattice pattern on the filling. Trim any overhanging pastry strips, pressing the ends down firmly on the rim of the pie. Use your thumb and index finger to create a wave pattern around the edge of the pastry. Whisk the egg yolk and milk and use this to brush over the pie, then sprinkle with the sugar. Bake the pie in the center of the oven for 40–45 minutes, until golden brown. This tastes best while still warm and served with yogurt.

Tip *Instead of using fresh blackberries, the recipe also works well with fresh raspberries or defrosted and well-drained berries.*

 | 🔌 *30 MINS* 🍱 *40–45 MINS* ❄ *30 MINS*

RAISIN BREAD

Moist Spelt Yeast Dough and a Hint of Orange

Raisins contain lots of minerals and B-group vitamins, so they are brilliant for combating physical exhaustion and stress. They taste particularly great in this classic north German recipe. In our version, we soak the raisins beforehand in orange juice so the bread is extra moist.

☞ *MAKES 1 LOAF*
(10 × 4¹/₂IN/
25 × 11CM)

YEAST DOUGH

1¹/₂ cups raisins

³/₄ cup orange juice

1 cup plus 1 tbsp milk of choice—we use almond milk, plus extra for brushing

2 tsp light honey

2 tbsp active dry yeast

pinch of salt

2 cups spelt flour, plus extra for dusting

1¹/₃ cups whole-grain spelt flour

4 tbsp softened butter, plus extra for greasing

1 large egg

Soak the raisins in the orange juice for 1 hour. Pour off the juice and leave to drain well.

To make the yeast dough, heat the milk in a pan until lukewarm. Add the honey, yeast, and salt and stir well until the yeast has completely dissolved. Use the dough hook attachment on an electric mixer to combine both types of flour with the yeast mixture, butter, and egg for a couple of minutes, until you have a glossy and supple dough. Work the raisins into the dough. Cover with a kitchen towel and leave to proof in a warm place for 1 hour, until doubled in volume.

Grease a loaf pan (10 × 4¹/₂in/11 × 25cm) with butter and dust with the flour. Knead the yeast dough once again on a floured work surface, shape it into a 10in (25cm) long roll, and transfer to the pan. Cover with a kitchen towel and leave to proof in a warm place for 30 minutes to 1 hour more, until it has significantly increased in volume.

Preheat the oven to 350°F (180°C). Brush the raisin bread with milk and make a roughly ¹/₂in (1cm) deep incision lengthwise along the loaf. Bake in the center of the oven for about 40 minutes, until risen and golden brown. After baking, let the raisin bread stand in the pan on a wire rack for about 10 minutes, then run a knife around the bread, take it out of the pan, and leave to cool completely.

 Tip *If you don't like raisins, you could replace them with dried cranberries or sour cherries. Currants and sultanas are also great options. Make sure you buy unsulfured dried fruit.*

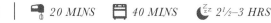 🔨 *20 MINS*   🍴 *40 MINS*   💤 *2¹/₂–3 HRS*

MINI CHOCOLATE CAKES

Molten Center, Dates, and Raspberry Coulis

Dark chocolate with a high cocoa content inhibits the release of stress hormones thanks to the flavonoids it contains, which means it has a calming effect. So every now and then, we love to treat ourselves to this pure indulgence with its molten center, sweet dates, and fresh fall fruits.

☞ *MAKES 6 MINI CAKES*

CAKE MIX

3$^{1}/_{2}$oz (100g) dried dates, finely chopped

3$^{1}/_{2}$oz (100g) dark chocolate, 70 percent cocoa content, coarsely chopped

1 tbsp cocoa powder, plus extra for dusting

2–3 drops vanilla extract

$^{1}/_{4}$ cup mild coconut oil, plus extra for greasing

2 large eggs

$^{1}/_{3}$ cup chickpea flour

RASPBERRY COULIS

5oz (150g) frozen raspberries, defrosted

$^{1}/_{2}$ tbsp dark brown sugar

ALSO

6 figs, stalks removed

2$^{1}/_{2}$oz (75g) blackberries

1$^{1}/_{2}$oz (40g) blueberries

1 tbsp pomegranate seeds

purple basil leaves and flowers (optional)

dark chocolate, 70 percent cocoa content (optional)

Place the dates in a pan with 5 tablespoons of water, bring them to a boil, and simmer gently until soft. Purée and leave to cool.

Preheat the oven to 350°F (180°C). Melt the chocolate over a double boiler along with the cocoa powder, vanilla extract, and coconut oil, stirring thoroughly. Leave the mixture to cool slightly.

Beat the eggs in a bowl with an electric mixer for several minutes, then add the date and chocolate mixture and stir. Finally, add the chickpea flour and continue to stir briefly. Grease the cups of a muffin pan with coconut oil and dust with cocoa powder. Divide the mixture evenly between the cups and bake in the center of the oven for 10–12 minutes, until risen.

Meanwhile, for the coulis, purée the raspberries with the sugar and push the mixture through a sieve. Make a cross-shaped incision in each fig and press it open like a crown. Serve the warm mini chocolate cakes immediately with the raspberry coulis, berries, and figs. If you wish, decorate with pomegranate seeds, basil leaves, and flowers, plus some grated chocolate.

Tip To make a lactose-free version, you can use vegan dark chocolate.

🍳 *20 MINS*   🍞 *10–12 MINS*

PLUM AND POPPY SEED TART

Crisp Spelt Shortcrust and Vanilla-Quark Filling

This tart is reminiscent of a favorite dish from our childhood days: quark soufflé with plums. We've packaged up the whole combination with a new twist to include poppy seeds and a vanilla custard—all in a heavenly tart with spelt shortcrust; light, low-fat quark; and a delicate hint of citrus.

☞ MAKES 1 TART
(DIAMETER
12IN/30CM)

SHORTCRUST PASTRY

1¹/₃ cups whole-grain spelt flour
  or whole-grain emmer or
  einkorn, plus extra for dusting

¹/₄ cup dark brown sugar

pinch of salt

7 tbsp cold butter, plus extra
  for greasing

1 large egg

baking beans, for blind baking

FILLING

1¹/₄ cups low-fat quark

¹/₂ cup full-fat cream cheese

3 large eggs

grated zest of 1 organic lemon

5 tbsp light honey

¹/₃ cup cornstarch

drop of vanilla extract

2 tbsp poppy seeds

1lb 2oz (500g) plums or
  damsons, halved and pits
  removed

Combine the flour, sugar, and salt in a bowl. Add the butter in little blobs and rub everything together with your fingers to form fine crumbs. Add the egg and work in quickly. Avoid overhandling the pastry; it should remain fairly lumpy. Wrap in plastic wrap and chill in the fridge for 30 minutes.

To make the filling, mix all the ingredients (except the plums) until the consistency is smooth and creamy.

Preheat the oven to 350°F (180°C). Grease a tart pan (diameter 12in/30cm) and dust with the flour. Roll out the pastry on a floured work surface into a large circle (diameter 14–15in/36–38cm). Transfer into the tart pan, press the edges down slightly, and trim off any overhanging pastry. Prick the pastry base several times with a fork and chill for 15 minutes. Line the pastry with parchment paper, fill with baking beans, and blind bake in the center of the oven for 20 minutes. Take the pastry crust out of the oven and remove the baking beans and parchment paper.

Spread the quark mixture evenly over the base and top with the plums, packed in close together (cut surface facing up). Cook the tart for 30–35 minutes, until done. Leave to cool before serving.

Tip *Instead of standard plums, you can also use other varieties of plums, such as greengages or Mirabelle plums.*

 30 MINS   📇 50–55 MINS   ❄ 45 MINS

CHICKPEA PANCAKES

Bay Leaf–Infused Pears and Almonds

If you enjoy warm pancakes for breakfast during the colder months, you will absolutely love this version with bay leaf–infused stewed pears and almonds. The chickpea flour makes the pancakes crisp on the outside and soft on the inside—and they are really filling.

☞ *MAKES 16–18 PANCAKES*

BATTER

¾ cup gluten-free rolled oats

2 large eggs

1 tbsp dark brown sugar

1 cup plus 1 tbsp almond milk

2 tbsp mild coconut oil, warmed, plus extra for cooking

2–3 drops vanilla extract

⅔ cup chickpea flour

1 tsp ground cinnamon

1 tsp baking powder

pinch of salt

ALSO

⅓ cup almonds

2 tbsp mild coconut oil

2 ripe, but still firm, pears (such as Williams), quartered and cored

2 fresh bay leaves

7oz (200g) blackberries

maple syrup (optional)

Grind the oats in a food processor to form a flour. Whisk together the eggs, sugar, milk, oil, and vanilla extract in a bowl. In another bowl, combine the ground oats, chickpea flour, cinnamon, baking powder, and salt. Add this to the egg mixture and beat everything using an electric mixer until you have a thick, smooth batter.

Toast the almonds in a dry pan over medium heat until pale brown. Remove from the pan and set aside. Heat the oil in the pan and add the quartered pears and bay leaves. Cook over medium heat for 4–5 minutes, turning the pears occasionally. Remove from the pan and set aside, remembering to remove the bay leaves before eating.

Heat some more oil in the pan and add 2 tablespoons of the batter for each pancake. Cook for 2–3 minutes, until the underside looks golden brown and firm, then flip the pancakes and continue cooking until the other side is also golden. Continue in this way until all the batter has been used, keeping the cooked pancakes warm as you work.

Serve the pancakes with the bay leaf–infused pears and blackberries. Coarsely chop the toasted almonds and scatter over and, if you wish, drizzle the pancakes with maple syrup.

20 MINS   25 MINS

GRAPE CALZONE

Honey, Olive Oil, and Rosemary

A trip to Tuscany inspired us to create this recipe. The combination of sweet Chianti grapes with rosemary and olive oil is really popular there. In this rustic calzone made using spelt flour, the earthy flavor of rosemary blends perfectly with the sweetness of the grapes and honey.

☞ *MAKES 6 CALZONE*

YEAST DOUGH

$^2/_3$ cup milk of choice—we use almond milk

2 tbsp dark brown sugar

$1^1/_2$ tsp active dry yeast

pinch of salt

$1^1/_2$ cups spelt flour, plus extra for dusting

2 tbsp mild olive oil, plus extra for brushing

FILLING

12oz (360g) black grapes, halved lengthwise and seeded

2 sprigs of rosemary

1 tbsp mild olive oil

1 tbsp white wine

1 tbsp light honey

grated zest of 1 organic lemon

DECORATION

sprig of rosemary, stems removed, needles finely chopped

To make the yeast dough, heat the milk in a pan until lukewarm. Add the sugar, yeast, and salt and stir well until the yeast has completely dissolved. Use the dough hook on an electric mixer to combine the flour, yeast mixture, and oil in a bowl for a couple of minutes, until you have a glossy, supple dough. Cover with a kitchen towel and leave to proof in a warm place for 1 hour, until doubled in volume.

Meanwhile, mix the grapes with the other filling ingredients.

Knead the dough again on a floured work surface and divide into 6 equal-sized portions. Shape these into balls and roll them out into circles (diameter about 6in/15cm). Spread some of the filling over half of each circle, leaving at least $^1/_2$in (1cm) free at the edge. Fold the pastry over the filling to create a semicircle shape. Press the air out from the center toward the edge, press down firmly all the way around, and crimp the edges to ensure the dough parcels are well-sealed. Transfer onto a sheet lined with parchment paper, cover with a kitchen towel, and leave to proof in a warm place for 30 minutes more. Decorate some of the calzone parcels with rosemary needles.

Preheat the oven to 400°F (200°C). Brush the calzone with a bit of oil and bake in the center of the oven for 10–12 minutes.

Tip   *To make a vegan version, the light honey can be replaced by the same quantity of maple syrup and the cow's milk with a plant-based milk.*

 20 MINS   *10–12 MINS*   *90 MINS*

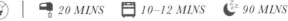

UPSIDE-DOWN CAKE

Figs and Hazelnuts

Figs might seem a little exotic, but new varieties are becoming available that can temporarily withstand temperatures of -20°F (-6°C), which means they can be cultivated in colder climates. We love this low-calorie fruit, which delivers dietary fiber along with vitamins and minerals.

☞ *MAKES 1 CAKE (DIAMETER 10½IN/26CM)*

CAKE MIXTURE

½ cup dark brown sugar

⅔ cup applesauce (see page 192)

¾ cup almond milk

1 tbsp cider or red wine vinegar

1 tsp ground cinnamon

2 cups spelt flour, plus extra for dusting

1 cup ground hazelnuts or almonds

5 tsp baking powder

pinch of salt

7 figs (about 14oz–1lb/ 400–450g), stalks removed, cut into ⅓in (7mm) thick slices

vegetable oil, for the pan

coconut yogurt, to serve

Preheat the oven to 350°F (180°C). In a bowl, briefly whisk the sugar, applesauce, almond milk, vinegar, and cinnamon using an electric mixer. In a second bowl, combine the flour, hazelnuts, baking powder, and salt, taking care to mix thoroughly. Add the liquid ingredients to this bowl and mix everything quickly until you have a smooth consistency.

Grease a springform pan (diameter 10½in/26cm) with oil and dust with the flour. Arrange the sliced figs on the base of the springform pan. Spread the cake mix over the top and bake in the center of the oven for 30–35 minutes, until risen and golden brown. When a toothpick inserted comes out clean, the cake is ready. Remove the fig cake from the oven and leave to cool slightly, then release from the pan and leave to cool upside down on a wire rack. This goes beautifully with coconut yogurt.

 Tip *You can also make this upside-down cake outside of fig season using halved apricots, plums, or slices of pear.*

🍳 🥄 🥣 | 🔌 *15 MINS* 🍞 *30–35 MINS*

Williams

Comice

Santa Maria

Alexander Lucas

Gute Luise

Conference

Beurre Hardy

Abate Fetel

Apple quince

Pear quince

QUINCE RYE CAKE

Blackberries and Walnuts

Thankfully, the once-overlooked quince is now being rediscovered. It is low in calories, rich in vitamin C, and was held in high regard by our grandmothers, who would have used it to make quince cheese and quince cake. Here, we combine it with blackberries and walnuts to make a really special sheet cake.

☞ *MAKES 1 SHEET CAKE*

YEAST DOUGH

³/₄ cup milk of choice—we use almond milk

2 tbsp dark brown sugar

1 tbsp active dry yeast

pinch of salt

1¹/₃ cups spelt flour, plus extra for dusting

1 cup rye flour

4 tbsp softened butter

FRUIT TOPPING

¹/₂ vanilla bean, sliced lengthwise and seeds removed

1 cup plus 1 tbsp unfiltered apple juice

3 tbsp maple syrup (or honey)

1 cinnamon stick

4 cloves

¹/₄ tsp black cardamom seeds

grated zest and 3 tbsp juice from 1 organic lemon

2¹/₄lb (1kg) quinces, peeled, quartered, and sliced into segments

¹/₃ cup walnuts

9oz (250g) blackberries (fresh or frozen and thawed)

To make the yeast dough, heat the milk in a pan until lukewarm. Add the sugar, yeast, and salt and stir well until the yeast has completely dissolved. Use the dough hook attachment on an electric mixer to combine both types of flour with the yeast mixture and the butter in a bowl for a couple of minutes, until you have a glossy and supple dough. Cover with a kitchen towel and leave to proof in a warm place for 1 hour, until doubled in volume.

Meanwhile, add the vanilla bean and seeds to a pan with the apple juice, 1 cup plus 1 tablespoon of water, maple syrup, spices, and lemon zest and juice and bring to a boil. Add the quinces and simmer for 10 minutes, until soft, then leave to drain. Retain the cooking liquid and simmer down until you have about ¹/₂ cup.

Preheat the oven to 350°F (185°C). Knead the yeast dough once more on a floured work surface and roll it out to the size of your sheet. Transfer it onto the sheet, lined with parchment paper, and top with a closely packed layer of quince slices. Drizzle with half the cooking liquid. Partially bake in the center of the oven for 15 minutes. Remove the cake from the oven and scatter over the walnuts and blackberries, then continue baking for another 20 minutes. Remove from the oven, drizzle over the remaining cooking liquid, and leave to cool.

Tip *For a vegan version, use the same quantity of mild coconut oil instead of the butter.*

🌀 | 📌 *35 MINS*   🍴 *35 MINS*   💤 *1 HR*

PEAR AND WALNUT BUNDT CAKE

Einkorn, Cardamom, and Cinnamon

Walnuts are packed with potassium and zinc, and their slightly bitter flavor goes beautifully with the vitamin-rich, sweet pears. When these two are combined with einkorn flour, the result is a moist cake, which will no doubt become a big favorite. A nice hot cup of tea provides the perfect accompaniment.

☞ *MAKES 1 BUNDT CAKE (DIAMETER 8½IN/22CM)*

CAKE MIXTURE

5 large eggs

³/₄ cup dark brown sugar

1 cup plus 1 tbsp mild vegetable oil, plus extra for greasing

¹/₂ tsp black cardamom seeds

3¹/₄ cups einkorn flour, plus extra for dusting

1 tsp ground cinnamon

5 tsp baking powder

pinch of salt

²/₃ cup milk of choice—we use almond milk

1 tbsp rum

2 pears, about 7oz (200g), peeled, cored, and chopped into small pieces

¹/₂ cup walnuts, chopped

ICING

1 batch cashew icing (see page 193)

DECORATION

walnut kernels, horned violets, purple basil leaves (optional)

Preheat the oven to 350°F (180°C). Beat the eggs and sugar in a bowl for several minutes with an electric mixer, gradually adding the oil as you go. Finely grind the cardamom using a pestle and mortar. In a second bowl, combine the cardamom, flour, cinnamon, baking powder, and salt, then add this in batches to the egg mixture, alternating with the milk and rum. Stir everything gently. Fold the chopped pears and nuts gently into the cake mixture.

Grease a bundt pan (diameter 8¹/₂in/22cm) with oil and dust with the flour. Pour the mixture into your pan and bake in the center of the oven for 50 minutes to 1 hour, until risen and golden brown. When a toothpick inserted comes out clean, the bundt cake is ready.

Leave to cool in the pan for about 10 minutes, then turn out onto a wire rack and leave to cool completely. Cover with the cashew icing and, if you wish, decorate with walnut kernels, horned violets, and basil leaves.

 You can also make a version of this bundt cake using chopped quince. Other nuts such as hazelnuts or almonds work well, too.

🕐 | 🍴 *15 MINS*   📟 *50–60 MINS*

QUINCE GALETTES

Crunchy Hazelnut Shortcrust and Applesauce

Not only do quinces have a unique flavor, they also have an unrivaled, aromatic scent with hints of citrus, pear, and apple. This low-calorie fruit will strengthen your immune system thanks to the valuable nutrients it contains. These French-style galettes are made using teff flour and hazelnuts and are simple yet simultaneously sophisticated.

☞ *MAKES 8 GALETTES*

SHORTCRUST PASTRY

1 cup teff flour, plus extra for dusting

²/₃ cup cornstarch

¹/₂ cup ground hazelnuts

2 tbsp dark brown sugar

pinch of salt

6 tbsp cold butter

¹/₄ cup buttermilk

1 large egg

FRUIT TOPPING

10oz (300g) quinces, peeled, quartered, and cored

1¹/₄ cups applesauce (see page 192)

GLAZE

1 tsp cornstarch

¹/₄ cup unfiltered apple juice

pinch of ground cinnamon

1–2 drops vanilla extract

Combine the teff flour, cornstarch, hazelnuts, sugar, and salt in a bowl. Add the butter in little blobs and rub everything together with your fingers to form fine crumbs. Add the buttermilk and egg and work in quickly. Avoid overhandling the pastry; it should remain fairly lumpy. Wrap in plastic wrap and chill in the fridge for 20 minutes.

Meanwhile, for the topping, slice the quinces very thinly using a potato peeler.

Preheat the oven to 350°F (185°C). On a floured work surface, divide the pastry into 8 equal-sized portions and shape each into a ball. Roll out the balls to make circles (diameter 5¹/₂in/14cm) and place them on two baking sheets lined with parchment paper. Put a portion of applesauce on each galette, leaving a ¹/₂in (1cm) border free around the edges. Top with the quince slices, overlapping the pieces in the shape of a rosette. Fold the edges of the pastry over the filling and press gently into place. Bake each sheet of galettes in the center of the oven for 25–30 minutes, until golden brown, then remove from the oven.

For the glaze, mix the cornstarch with 1 tablespoon of the apple juice. Bring the remaining apple juice, cinnamon, and vanilla extract to a boil in a pan. Add the cornstarch paste while stirring constantly and continue to simmer briefly until the glaze has thickened. Brush the glaze over the galettes while they are still warm and serve.

Tip *Of course, this recipe also tastes great with apple or pear slices.*

🖐 25 MINS   🍳 50–60 MINS   ❄ 20 MINS

Rhubarb

Chickpeas

Kidney beans

Heritage carrots

Beet

Parsnip

Zucchini

Hokkaido squash

Butternut squash

PARSNIP CAKE

Coconut, Raisins, and Cream Cheese Topping

Parsnips are usually cooked in savory dishes and are not often used as an ingredient in baking. Nevertheless, this vegetable, which is rich in the micronutrients niacin and potassium, has a perfect flavor for sweet cakes.

☞ *MAKES 1 CAKE (DIAMETER 8IN/20CM)*

CAKE MIXTURE

¹/₂ cup mild coconut oil, plus extra for greasing

2 large eggs

³/₄ cup dark brown sugar

2–3 drops vanilla extract

1 cup whole-grain einkorn flour, plus extra for dusting

¹/₂ cup shredded coconut

1 tsp ground cinnamon

1 tsp pumpkin pie spice

2 tsp baking powder

pinch of salt

²/₃ cup milk of choice—we use almond milk

1 tbsp rum

6oz (175g) parsnips, peeled and finely grated

¹/₂ cup raisins

TOPPING

7oz (200g) full-fat cream cheese

3 tbsp runny honey

2 tbsp mild coconut oil

grated zest of 1 organic lemon

2 tbsp toasted coconut flakes

Preheat the oven to 350°F (185°C). Gently melt the coconut oil in a pan over low heat. Beat the eggs and sugar in a bowl for several minutes with an electric mixer, gradually adding the melted coconut oil and vanilla extract as you go. In another bowl, combine the flour, shredded coconut, spices, baking powder, and salt. Add this in batches to the egg and oil mixture, alternating with the milk and rum and stirring everything gently. Fold the grated parsnips and raisins into the cake mix.

Grease a springform pan (diameter 8in/20cm) with coconut oil and dust with the flour. Pour the cake mix into the pan, smooth the surface, and bake in the center of the oven for 35–40 minutes, until risen and golden brown. When a toothpick inserted comes out clean, the cake is ready. Leave the cake to cool in the pan for about 10 minutes, then turn out onto a wire rack and leave to cool completely.

To make the topping, briefly beat the cream cheese, honey, coconut oil, and lemon zest with an electric mixer until creamy. Spread the cream evenly over the cake and sprinkle with coconut flakes.

 *25 MINS*   *35–40 MINS*

FRESH FROM
THE OVEN

When the first snow envelops the countryside in
a white cloak and the garden goes into winter
hibernation, we make ourselves cosy indoors with
a warming mug of tea. To boost our spirits, nothing
can beat a sweet pastry with beets, cranberries, and
fine spices, still warm from the oven.

MINI FRUIT PIES

With Apple and Cranberry Filling

If we had to find another term to convey the meaning of "comfort," we would definitely opt for "pie." As the weather gets cooler, what could be better than baking these sweet and satisfying individual pies to be enjoyed with a warm drink?

☞ *MAKES 18 PIES*

SHORTCRUST PASTRY

$^{1}/_{2}$ cup mild coconut oil

$^{3}/_{4}$ cup whole-grain spelt, emmer, or einkorn flour

1 cup spelt flour, plus extra for dusting

2 tsp dark brown sugar

pinch of salt

FILLING

$5^{1}/_{2}$ oz (165g) apples (about 2 small apples), peeled, quartered, cored, and cut into small pieces

3oz (80g) frozen cranberries, thawed

1 tbsp dark brown sugar

2 tsp ground cinnamon

1 tbsp lemon juice

ALSO

2 tbsp plant-based milk

1 tbsp dark brown sugar

Melt the coconut oil in a pan over low heat and set aside for about 15 minutes. Combine both types of flour, the sugar, and salt in a bowl. Add the coconut oil and quickly rub the ingredients together. Avoid overhandling the pastry; it should remain fairly lumpy. Add $^{1}/_{4}$ cup of water and continue to work briefly. Wrap the pastry in plastic wrap and chill in the fridge for 20 minutes.

Meanwhile, to make the filling, bring the chopped apples, cranberries, $^{1}/_{2}$ cup of water, and the remaining filling ingredients to a boil in a pan. Lower the heat and simmer everything for 5–7 minutes, until the cranberries have split open. Leave the filling to cool.

Preheat the oven to 350°F (180°C). Roll out the shortcrust on a floured work surface until $^{1}/_{8}$–$^{1}/_{4}$in (3–5mm) thick and cut out rounds ($3^{1}/_{4}$in/8cm in diameter) with a cookie cutter. Place half of the pastry rounds on two baking sheets lined with parchment paper. For the lids, use a piping bag nozzle or a thimble to cut out 3 little circles in the remaining pastry rounds. Alternatively, make 3 little incisions in the lids using a knife. Place the filling in the center of the pie bases, leaving a $^{1}/_{2}$in (1cm) border all the way around. Place the pie lids on top, press down the edges firmly, and use a fork to seal them in place. Brush the hand pies with the milk and sprinkle with the sugar. Bake each sheet in the center of the oven for 25–30 minutes, until golden brown.

25 MINS   *50–60 MINS*   *20 MINS*

SCONES

Apple and Hazelnut—Cherry and Vanilla—Rose Hip

Scones are perfect whatever the occasion—not just as a breakfast treat. They are simply unbeatable, particularly if served fresh from the oven with a cup of coffee. In this recipe, we would like to introduce you to our three favorite and rather unusual versions.

☞ *MAKES 8 SCONES*

VERSION 1

$^{1}/_{2}$ cup hazelnuts

$3^{1}/_{2}$oz (100g) apples (about $^{1}/_{2}$ apple), peeled, cored, and finely diced

$^{1}/_{2}$ tsp ground cinnamon

VERSION 2

$^{1}/_{2}$ cup dried sour cherries

$^{1}/_{4}$ cup apple juice

2–3 drops vanilla extract

VERSION 3

$^{1}/_{2}$ cup dried rose hips, chopped

$^{1}/_{4}$ cup orange juice

BASIC SCONE MIX

$1^{1}/_{3}$ cups spelt flour, plus extra for dusting

2 tsp baking powder

3 tsp dark brown sugar

pinch of salt

4 tbsp cold butter

$^{2}/_{3}$ cup buttermilk

some milk for brushing

honey, clotted cream, butter, and jam, to serve

VERSION 1   Toast the hazelnuts in a dry pan. Leave to cool, then chop. Combine the hazelnuts, diced apples, and cinnamon.

VERSION 2   Soak the sour cherries in the apple juice for 1 hour. Pour away the juice and leave to drain well. Add the vanilla extract.

VERSION 3   Soak the rose hips in the orange juice for 1 hour. Pour off the juice and leave to drain well.

BASIC SCONE MIX   Preheat the oven to 425°F (220°C). Combine the flour, baking powder, sugar, and salt in a bowl. Add the butter in little blobs and rub everything together by hand to form crumbs. Add the buttermilk and work it in quickly. Fold your chosen preprepared fruit or nut and fruit combination into the basic scone mix.

Roll out the scone dough on a floured work surface until it is roughly $^{3}/_{4}$–$1^{1}/_{2}$in (2–3cm) thick. Cut out circles ($2^{1}/_{2}$in/6cm in diameter) with a cookie cutter and place upside down on a baking sheet lined with parchment paper. Brush with milk and bake in the center of the oven for 9–12 minutes, until the scones have risen nicely and are golden brown. Serve while still warm. These go wonderfully with honey, clotted cream, butter, and jam.

🕐 | 🔨 *10 MINS*   🍞 *9–12 MINS*   💤 *IF APPLICABLE, 1 HR*

BEET BUNDT CAKE

Poppy Seeds, Vanilla, and Pear

The inspiration for this fantastic recipe came from some freshly squeezed juice made using beets, pears, and celery. The earthy tones of the beets mingle with the fruity pear and the poppy seeds to give this charming food pairing a wonderful nuttiness. The whole ensemble is just as convincing in bundt cake form!

☞ MAKES 1 BUNDT
CAKE (DIAMETER
8½IN/22CM)

CAKE MIXTURE

5 large eggs

²/₃ cup maple syrup

1 cup plus 1 tbsp mild vegetable
oil, plus extra for greasing

2–3 drops vanilla extract

1¹/₃ cups almond flour, plus
extra for dusting

1¹/₃ cups cornstarch

scant 1oz (25g) poppy seeds

5 tsp baking powder

pinch of salt

1 cup plus 1 tbsp almond milk

2 tbsp rum

3oz (80g) beets

¹/₂ pear, about 3oz/80g,
peeled, cored, and cut into
small pieces

ICING

1 batch cashew icing
(see page 193)

2 tsp beet powder

ALSO

¹/₂ tsp poppy seeds, to decorate

Preheat the oven to 350°F (180°C). Beat the eggs and maple syrup in a bowl for several minutes with an electric mixer, gradually adding the oil and vanilla extract. In a second bowl, combine the almond flour, cornstarch, poppy seeds, baking powder, and salt. Add this in batches to the egg mixture, alternating with the almond milk and rum and mixing everything gently.

Place the beets in a pan of water and bring to a boil. Lower the heat and simmer for 45–60 minutes, until soft. Drain, submerge in cold water, peel, leave to cool, and grate coarsely or finely dice. Carefully fold the beets and pear into the cake mix.

Grease a bundt pan (diameter 8½in/22cm) with oil and dust with the flour. Pour the cake mix into the pan and bake in the center of the oven for about 1 hour, until the cake has risen and is golden brown. When a toothpick inserted comes out clean, the bundt cake is ready. Leave to cool in the pan for about 10 minutes, then turn out onto a wire rack and leave to cool completely.

Color the cashew icing with beet powder and use to decorate the cake. Scatter over the poppy seeds.

 20 MINS | 1 HR

FIG AND WALNUT BARS

Fig Filling and Nutty Crust

When everyday stress is getting you down, what you need is a quick snack. To make sure you really get an energy boost, we have created this healthier muesli bar with three layers: base, fruit filling, and crunchy nut topping. It's the ideal power snack to keep you going!

☞ *MAKES 12 BARS*

BASE

1 tbsp flax seeds

1 cup walnuts

$1/4$ cup hazelnuts

$2^1/4$ cups gluten-free
  rolled oats

$1/4$ cup applesauce
  (see page 192)

2 tbsp maple syrup

1 tbsp mild coconut oil, plus
  extra for greasing

2–3 drops vanilla extract

$1/2$ tsp baking powder

pinch of salt

FILLING

2 cups dried figs, coarsely
  chopped

2–3 drops vanilla extract

$1/2$ cup applesauce
  (see page 192)

grated zest of 1 organic orange

1 cup walnuts, coarsely
  chopped

$1/4$ cup hazelnuts, coarsely
  chopped

Grind the flax seeds for the base using a pestle and mortar. Combine with $1/4$ cup of water in a small bowl and leave to swell for 15 minutes, until the mixture has a gel-like consistency.

Meanwhile, preheat the oven to 350°F (180°C). Lightly toast the walnuts and hazelnuts in a dry pan until pale brown. Leave the nuts to cool completely. Grind half of the oats in a food processor to make a coarse flour. Add the toasted walnuts and hazelnuts and pulse briefly until the mixture has been ground to a sandy texture. Add the flax seed gel, applesauce, maple syrup, coconut oil, and vanilla extract and pulse briefly in the food processor until the mixture has come together. Transfer into a large bowl and combine by hand with the remaining oats, baking powder, and salt. Grease a square baking pan (8 × 8in/20 × 20cm) with coconut oil. Put two-thirds of the mixture into the pan and press down firmly with damp hands.

To make the filling, put the figs in the food processor. Add the vanilla extract, applesauce, and orange zest and process until you have a fine paste. Spread this fig paste over the mixture and smooth the surface. Cover the filling with the remaining base mixture. Scatter the walnuts and hazelnuts over, making sure they are evenly distributed and covering the whole surface, then press gently into the fig mixture. Bake in the center of the oven for 25–30 minutes, until the top is a pale golden-brown color. Leave to cool completely before cutting into 12 bars. If stored in an airtight container and refrigerated, the fig and walnut bars will keep for up to 5 days.

🌾 🌿 🥜 🍊 | 📠 *25 MINS*   🍳 *25–30 MINS*

BUILDING BLOCKS: BANANA BREAD

One Loaf—Lots of Options

☞ *FOR 1 LOAF (LOAF PAN 4½ × 10IN/11 × 25CM)*

① THE BASIC INGREDIENTS

2 tbsp flax seeds, crushed
1¾ cups gluten-free rolled oats
1 cup spelt flour, plus extra for dusting
2 tsp baking powder
pinch of salt
1 cup dried dates, finely chopped
⅔ cup almond milk
2–3 drops vanilla extract
1 tbsp cider vinegar
3 large bananas, peeled and mashed
+ 1 banana for decoration
vegetable oil, for greasing

Preheat the oven to 350°F (180°C). Stir the flax seeds into 6 tablespoons of water and leave to swell for 15 minutes, until the mixture has a gel-like consistency. Grind the oats in a food processor to make flour. Combine the ground oats, spelt flour, baking powder, and salt in a bowl. Pulse the dates, almond milk, vanilla extract, and cider vinegar in a food processor until you have a fine mixture. Stir in the mashed bananas and flax seed gel. Add this mixture to the dry ingredients and mix well.

② SOME CRUNCH

½ cup walnuts, chopped
or
⅓ cup almonds, chopped
or
½ cup hazelnuts, chopped
or
½ cup cashews, chopped
or
½ cup Brazil nuts, chopped
or
⅓ cup peanuts, chopped

Optionally add your chosen chopped nuts to the mixture.

③ ADDED FLAVOR

2½oz (75g) carrot, grated
or
2½oz (75g) zucchini, grated
or
2½oz (75g) apple, grated
or
2½oz (75g) dark chocolate (70 percent cocoa content)
or
2½oz (75g) blackberries
or
2½oz (75g) strawberries

Add your flavoring of choice and mix well.

🌱 🥛 🌾 | ⎯ *20 MINS*   ▢ *60–70 MINS*

PREPARATION AND BAKING

Grease a loaf pan ($4^{1}/_{2}$ × 10in/11 × 25cm) and dust with the flour. Transfer the mixture to the pan and smooth the surface. Peel the banana, slice in half lengthwise, and place both halves, cut surface facing upward, on top of the loaf. Bake the bread in the center of the oven for 60–70 minutes, until risen and golden. When a toothpick inserted comes out clean, the loaf is cooked. Leave to cool in the pan for 10 minutes, then turn it out and leave to cool completely.

BROWNIES

Kidney Beans, Maple Syrup, and Vanilla

It might be unusual to bake brownies using kidney beans, but not only are beans "low carb" and very rich in protein, they also make the brownies super moist. And the flavor of the beans doesn't stand out—instead, you get the usual delicious chocolate taste!

 MAKES 16 BROWNIES

THE BROWNIE MIX

$1^{3}/_{4}$ cups kidney beans (drained weight)

$^{1}/_{3}$ cup mild coconut oil, plus extra for greasing

$^{1}/_{2}$ cup gluten-free rolled oats

$^{1}/_{4}$ cup cocoa powder, plus extra for dusting

$^{1}/_{4}$ cup nut butter (cashew or almond)

$^{2}/_{3}$ cup maple syrup

$^{1}/_{4}$ cup almond milk

2–3 drops vanilla extract

1 tsp baking powder

pinch of salt

$2^{1}/_{2}$oz (75g) dark chocolate, 70 percent cocoa content, chopped

Preheat the oven to 350°F (185°C). Drain the beans well and rinse in cold water. Use a food processor to purée all the ingredients, except the chocolate, until smooth. Then fold $^{1}/_{2}$ cup of the chocolate into the brownie mix. Grease a square baking pan (8 × 8in/20 × 20cm) with coconut oil and dust with cocoa powder. Pour the brownie mixture into the pan, smooth the surface, scatter over the remaining chocolate chunks, and bake for 35–40 minutes in the center of the oven. Leave the brownie to cool in the pan, then slice into 16 squares.

Tip   *To make a vegan version, you could use vegan dark chocolate.*

10 MINS   *35–40 MINS*

SQUASH MUFFINS

Walnuts and Olive Oil

We love pumpkin and squash recipes. This autumnal vegetable is healthy and unbelievably tasty—what's more, it is really versatile, low in calories, and packed with vitamins. The delicate pumpkin flesh makes these muffins beautifully moist, as well as providing plenty of dietary fiber and natural sweetness.

☞ *MAKES 18 MUFFINS*

MUFFIN MIXTURE

9oz (250g) pumpkin or squash flesh (such as Hokkaido or butternut), peel left on, diced

2 large eggs

$^1/_2$ cup dark brown sugar

$^1/_4$ cup mild olive oil

$^1/_4$ cup milk of choice—we use almond milk

2 cloves

$^3/_4$ cup whole-grain spelt flour

1 cup spelt flour

2 tsp ground cinnamon

2 tsp baking powder

pinch of salt

$^1/_2$ cup walnuts, coarsely chopped

DECORATION

1 batch cashew icing (see page 193)

2 tsp fruit powder

edible flowers, such as rose, cornflowers, lavender (optional)

Cook the squash in a pan with $^2/_3$ cup of water for 15 minutes, until soft. Drain thoroughly, then purée in a blender. (It should produce about 7oz/200g.) Leave to cool.

Preheat the oven to 350°F (180°C). Beat the eggs and sugar in a bowl for several minutes with an electric mixer, until the mixture is a pale cream color. Add the oil and milk and stir in the puréed squash. Grind the cloves using a pestle and mortar. In a second bowl, combine both types of flour with the cinnamon, baking powder, and salt, then add in batches to the egg mixture.

Fold the walnuts into the mixture. Fill the cups of a muffin pan with 12 paper liners, divide the mixture evenly between the liners, and bake the muffins in the center of the oven for 20–22 minutes, until risen and golden brown. When a toothpick inserted comes out clean, the muffins are ready. Remove from the pan and leave to cool on a wire rack.

To decorate, color the cashew icing with the fruit powder. Ice the muffins and, if you wish, scatter with edible flowers.

🔌 *20 MINS*   🔲 *20–22 MINS*

BEET CAKE

Dark Chocolate and Chocolate Ganache

Outstanding baking results can also be achieved with root vegetables such as beets. This healthy tuber ensures everything stays beautifully moist and produces a superb deep red color. When combined with chocolate, the end result is a truly sumptuous culinary delight. The highlight is the ganache!

☞ **MAKES 1 CAKE (DIAMETER 8IN/20CM)**

CAKE MIXTURE

1lb (450g) beets

3 large eggs

pinch of salt

¹/₂ cup dark brown sugar

²/₃ cup mild vegetable oil, plus extra for greasing

2–3 drops vanilla extract

³/₄ cup whole-grain spelt flour, plus extra for dusting

¹/₄ cup cocoa powder

1 tsp baking powder

2¹/₂oz (75g) dark chocolate, 70 percent cocoa content

GANACHE

2 tbsp mild coconut oil

3 tbsp cocoa powder

1–2 drops vanilla extract

2 tbsp maple syrup

DECORATION

2 tsp beet powder

1oz (30g) dark chocolate, 70 percent cocoa content, coarsely chopped

Place the beets in a pan of water and bring to a boil. Lower the heat and simmer for 45–60 minutes, until soft. Drain, submerge in cold water, peel, leave to cool, and grate coarsely.

Preheat the oven to 350°F (180°C). Separate the eggs. Beat the egg whites and salt in a bowl with an electric mixer until stiff. In a second bowl, whisk the egg yolks and sugar, gradually adding the oil and vanilla extract. Combine the flour, cocoa powder, and baking powder. Add this to the egg yolk mixture and mix briefly. Chop the chocolate and melt over a double boiler. Fold the melted chocolate and beets into the cake mix. Finally, gently fold in the egg whites with a balloon whisk.

Grease a springform pan (diameter 8in/20cm) with oil and dust with the flour. Pour the mixture into your pan and bake the cake in the center of the oven for 45 minutes, until risen. When a toothpick inserted comes out clean, the cake is ready. Leave to cool on a wire rack.

To make the ganache, melt the ingredients over a double boiler, stir well, and spread evenly over the cake. Chill the cake in the fridge for 30 minutes, until the ganache has set. Dust the cake with beet powder and scatter over the chopped chocolate.

Tip *To make a lactose-free version, you can use vegan dark chocolate.*

 🔪 *25 MINS* 🍳 *45–60 MINS + 45 MINS* ❄ *30 MINS*

"ELISENLEBKUCHEN"

Almonds and Lebkuchen Spices

The story behind the traditional German cookie known as Elisenlebkuchen begins in Nuremberg, Germany, in 1395, when a baker named his "lebkuchen" cookie recipe after his daughter Elisabeth. Ever since, in Germany, these lebkuchen have been associated with the lead-up to Christmas, just like mulled wine and eggnog. This recipe is particularly delicious and moist thanks to the nuts and maple syrup.

☞ *MAKES 30 LEBKUCHEN*

THE DOUGH

2 large eggs

²/₃ cup maple syrup

¹/₂ tsp black cardamom seeds

6 cloves

2 whole allspice berries

3 tsp ground cinnamon

pinch of grated nutmeg

¹/₈oz (1g) fresh ginger, peeled and finely grated

grated zest of ¹/₂ organic orange

pinch of salt

1¹/₃ cups ground almonds

1 cup whole-grain spelt flour or whole-grain einkorn flour

¹/₂ tsp baking powder

ALSO

30 edible rice paper discs (diameter 2in/5cm)

Beat the eggs and maple syrup in a large bowl for several minutes with an electric mixer until foamy. Finely grind the cardamom, cloves, and allspice using a pestle and mortar. In a second bowl, combine the spices, ginger, orange zest, salt, almonds, flour, and baking powder. Add the dry ingredients in batches to the egg mixture and combine to make a smooth dough.

Place the rice paper discs on three sheets lined with parchment paper. Put a blob of the dough on each disc and use a moistened knife to spread the mixture into a slightly domed shape. Leave to rest for 1 hour. Preheat the oven to 350°F (180°C). Bake each sheet in the center of the oven for about 20 minutes, then remove and leave to cool on a wire rack.

Tip *If stored in an airtight container in a cool place, these will keep for 3–4 weeks.*

15 MINS | 1 HR | 1 HR

COURONNE

Sumptuous Yeast Wreath with a Date and Nut Filling

The couronne is a variant on the galette des rois that originates in the South of France. It is a filled yeast wreath, which also makes an ideal gift. We complement the yeasted spelt dough with a filling made from bitter walnuts and dried sour cherries, with added dates for a natural sweetness.

☞ *MAKES 1 COURONNE*

YEAST DOUGH

¹/₂ tsp black cardamom seeds

¹/₂ cup milk of choice—we use almond milk

2 tbsp light honey

1³/₄ tsp active dry yeast

pinch of salt

1¹/₃ cups spelt flour, plus extra for dusting

2 tbsp softened butter

FILLING

1 cup dried dates, finely chopped

²/₃ cup walnuts

¹/₂ tsp black cardamom seeds

1 tsp ground cinnamon

4 tbsp softened butter

2–3 drops vanilla extract

¹/₄ cup dried sour cherries

ALSO

1 tbsp milk of choice

1 egg yolk

Finely grind the cardamom seeds using a pestle and mortar. To make the yeast dough, heat the milk in a pan until lukewarm. Add the cardamom, honey, yeast, and salt and stir well until the yeast has completely dissolved. Use the dough hook on an electric mixer to combine the flour, yeast mixture, and butter in a bowl for a couple of minutes, until you have a glossy, supple dough. The dough may seem to be relatively soft, but this consistency is absolutely right. Cover with a kitchen towel and leave to proof in a warm place for 1 hour, until doubled in volume.

Meanwhile, for the filling, place the dates in a pan with ¹/₂ cup of water, bring them to a boil, then simmer gently until soft. Drain and leave to cool. Toast the walnuts in a dry pan and likewise leave to cool. Finely grind the cardamom seeds using a pestle and mortar. Pulse the dates, walnuts, and the spices in a food processor or blend using an electric mixer until you have a smooth paste. Add the butter and vanilla extract.

Knead the dough once again on a floured work surface and roll it out into a rectangle (about 20 × 10in/50 × 25cm). Spread the nut paste evenly over the surface. Scatter the sour cherries over the paste. Roll up the rectangle from the long side and cut it in half lengthwise with a sharp knife. Arrange the halves with the filling facing upward, join them together at one end, then twist together to create a braid. Join the two ends and lay the wreath on a sheet lined with parchment paper. Cover with a kitchen towel and leave to proof in a warm place for 30 minutes to 1 hour more, until it has significantly increased in volume.

Preheat the oven to 350°F (180°C). Whisk the milk and egg yolk and brush the mixture over the wreath. Bake in the center of the oven for 10–15 minutes, until the couronne has risen and is golden.

🕐 *20 MINS* 🍴 *10–15 MINS* 💤 *90 MINS TO 2 HRS*

PANETTONE

Hazelnuts and Dried Fruit

Panettone, a speciality from Milan, is traditionally baked at Christmas. We always feel the classic recipe is rather dry, so in our mini version, we soak the dried fruit beforehand to make them more moist. Hazelnuts and almonds ensure that essential crunch.

☞ *MAKES 12 MINI PANETTONE*

YEAST DOUGH

1 cup mixed dried fruit, such as figs, dates, sour cherries, raisins, and cranberries

3 tbsp rum

3 tbsp orange juice

1/2 cup milk of choice—we use almond milk

1/3 cup dark brown sugar

2–3 drops vanilla extract

1 tsp active dry yeast

pinch of salt

2 cups spelt flour, plus extra for dusting

7 tbsp softened butter

2 large eggs

grated zest of 1 organic orange and 1 organic lemon

1/2 cup hazelnuts, coarsely chopped

ALSO

1 tbsp milk of choice

1 egg yolk

2 tbsp sliced almonds

Ideally the night before or a couple of hours in advance, coarsely chop the dried fruit, transfer to a bowl, and pour over the rum and orange juice. Leave the mixture to soak for as long as possible.

To make the yeast dough, heat the milk in a pan until lukewarm. Add the sugar, vanilla extract, yeast, and salt and stir well until the yeast has dissolved. Use the dough hook on an electric mixer to combine the flour, yeast mixture, butter, eggs, and citrus fruit zest in a bowl for a couple of minutes, until you have a glossy, supple dough. The dough will appear very soft, but this is exactly the right consistency to ensure the panettone turn out beautifully moist. Cover with a kitchen towel and leave to proof in a warm place for 1 hour to 1 hour 30 minutes, until doubled in volume.

Fill the cups of a muffin pan with 12 paper liners. Drain the fruit. Work the hazelnuts and fruit into the dough. Working on a floured work surface, divide the dough into 12 portions using well-floured hands, shape each portion into a ball, and put each one into a muffin cup. Cover with a kitchen towel and leave to proof in a warm place for 20 minutes more.

Preheat the oven to 350°F (180°C). Whisk the milk and egg yolk and brush over the panettone, then sprinkle with the sliced almonds. Bake in the center of the oven for 15–20 minutes, until golden brown. The panettone taste best if eaten slightly warm.

Tip *If you unexpectedly end up with some panettone left over, you can use it to make delicious French toast!*

🖳 *15 MINS*   ▦ *15–20 MINS*   💤 *4–12 HRS + 110 MINS*

SPICED HONEY "LEBKUCHEN"

Almonds and Orange Zest

This is a favorite advent recipe in Germany, and here we bake it with wholesome spelt flour and almonds. The most important thing in terms of the flavor is to use plenty of freshly ground spices, orange zest, and honey. Instead of icing the cookies, we decorate them with almonds, pumpkin seeds, and cranberries.

☞ *MAKES ABOUT 40 LEBKUCHEN*

THE DOUGH

4 black peppercorns

4 whole allspice berries

6 cloves

1/2 tsp black cardamom seeds

pinch of grated nutmeg

1 tsp ground cinnamon

1/2 tsp ground ginger

1 1/4 cups honey

grated zest of 1 organic orange

4 cups whole-grain spelt flour, plus extra for dusting

1 cup ground almonds

1/2 cup almonds, chopped

5 tsp baking powder

pinch of salt

2 large eggs

DECORATION

some egg white

blanched almonds, pumpkin seeds, dried cranberries (as desired)

Finely grind the peppercorns, allspice, cloves, and cardamom using a pestle and mortar, then combine with the other spices. Briefly heat the honey, spices, and orange zest in a pan over low heat, stir, and set aside to cool.

Combine the flour, ground and chopped almonds, baking powder, and salt in a bowl. Add the honey mixture and the eggs, and process the ingredients for a couple of minutes using the dough hook attachment on an electric mixer to create a dough. Shape it into a ball, wrap in plastic wrap, and leave to rest for 30 minutes in the fridge.

Preheat the oven to 350°F (180°C). Roll out the dough on a floured work surface until approximately 2in (5mm) thick and cut out different shapes with a cookie cutter as desired. Place the lebkuchen spaced slightly apart on two baking sheets lined with parchment paper. Brush with egg white and decorate with your choice of almonds, pumpkin seeds, and dried cranberries. Bake each sheet in the center of the oven for about 10 minutes, until the edges are pale brown, then remove and leave to cool on a wire rack.

Tip *If stored in an airtight container in a cool place, the lebkuchen will keep for 4–5 weeks.*

🕐 | 🔨 *15 MINS*   🍞 *20 MINS*   💤 *30 MINS*

CRANBERRY CAKE

Almond-Coconut Sponge Cake and Coffee-Orange Cream

☞ *MAKES 1 CAKE*
(DIAMETER
8IN/20CM)

JAM

3¹/₂oz (100g) frozen and thawed
  cranberries

1¹/₂ tbsp maple syrup

CAKE MIX

4 large eggs

¹/₂ cup dark brown sugar

¹/₂ cup mild vegetable oil, plus
  extra for greasing

grated zest of 1 organic orange

1 cup almond flour, plus extra
  for dusting

¹/₄ cup shredded coconut

³/₄ cup cornstarch

3 tsp baking powder

pinch of salt

²/₃ cup almond milk

CREAM FILLING

1 tsp coffee beans

9³/₄oz (280g) full-fat
  cream cheese

¹/₃ cup almond butter

3 tbsp maple syrup

2–3 drops vanilla extract

DECORATION

1 tbsp shredded coconut

pink peppercorns, carnations,
  eucalyptus (optional)

Bring the cranberries to a boil in a pan with the maple syrup and ¹/₂ cup of water. When the berries burst open, lower the heat and simmer for 5 minutes. Remove the jam from the stove top and leave to cool. The jam will thicken considerably thanks to the natural pectin contained in the cranberries.

Preheat the oven to 350°F (180°C). Beat the eggs and sugar for several minutes in a bowl using an electric mixer. Gradually add the oil, then stir in half the orange zest. In a second bowl, combine the almond flour, shredded coconut, cornstarch, baking powder, and salt and add this in batches to the egg mixture, alternating with the almond milk and stirring gently. Grease two springform pans (diameter 8in/20cm) with oil and dust with almond flour. Divide the cake mixture equally between the pans, smooth the surface, and bake in the center of the oven for 20–25 minutes, until risen and golden brown. When a toothpick inserted comes out clean, the cakes are ready. Leave to cool on a wire rack.

To make the cream filling, finely grind the coffee beans using a pestle and mortar. Combine the ground coffee with the remaining ingredients and the rest of the orange zest by mixing briefly with an electric mixer.

Place one of the cakes on a cake platter and spread with the jam. Transfer the cream into a piping bag with a large round nozzle and pipe dollops of the jam on top. Place the second cake on top. Sprinkle shredded coconut over the cake and, if you wish, decorate with pink peppercorns, carnations, and eucalyptus. Chill the cake for at least 30 minutes in the fridge before serving.

30 MINS　*20–25 MINS*　❄ *30 MINS*

ALL ABOUT BAKING

When is each fruit or vegetable in season? Where can I track down einkorn or teff flour? Which foods are particularly recommended? We have the answers to these questions and more! On the following pages, you will find valuable tips about baking and information about different ingredients.

FRUIT	MARCH	APRIL	MAY	JUNE	JULY	AUG
Apples						
Apricots						
Pears						
Blackberries						
Cranberries						
Strawberries						
Figs						
Blueberries						
Raspberries, red						
Raspberries, yellow						
Elderberries						
Red currants						
Black currants						
White currants						
Mirabelle plums						
Nectarines						
Peaches						
Plums						
Plums, yellow						
Lingonberries						
Quinces						
Greengages						
Sour cherries						
Gooseberries						
Sweet cherries						
Wild strawberries						
Wild blueberries						
Grapes						
Damsons						

VEGETABLES	MARCH	APRIL	MAY	JUNE	JULY	AUG
Butternut squash						
Hokkaido squash						
Carrots						
Parsnip						
Rhubarb						
Beets						
Zucchini						

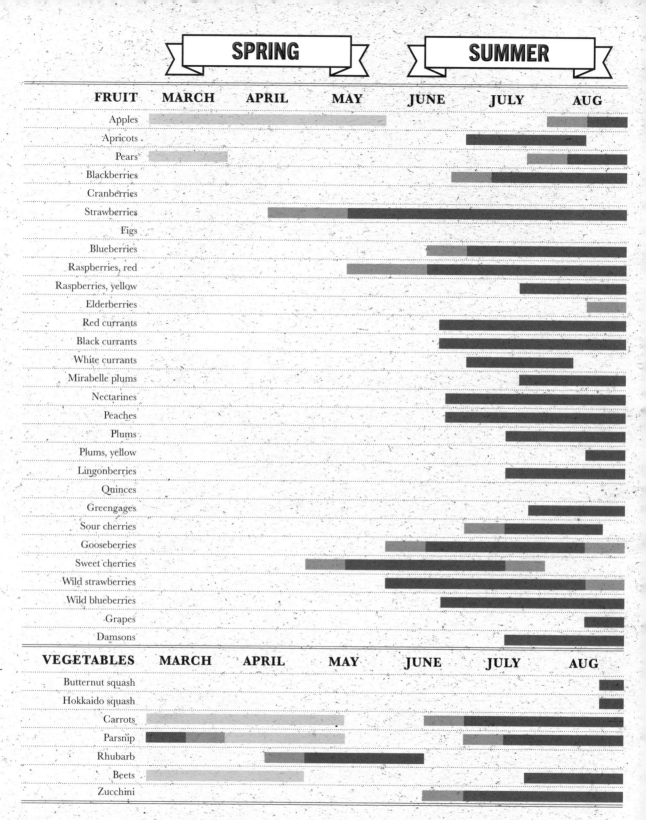

peak season for local cultivation   early / late season for local cultivation   stored goods locally cultivated   🍒 very early to late varieties

NATURAL COLORS

From Red to Purple, Organic Fruit Powders Provide Color

Beet

Black currant

Blueberry

Raspberry

Strawberry

Fruit powders are produced from freeze-dried berries or vegetables such as beets. After drying, these are ground without any other additives. The resulting intensely colored powders are perfect for adding natural color to cake mixtures and creams and are available in a wide variety of shades. Not only are these powders a healthier alternative to chemically manufactured food colorings, they also add flavor and can be used to refine the aroma of the end product. We like using fruit powders to color cashew icing (see page 193), which we use instead of sugar frosting. Or we dust cookies, cakes, and so on with colorful powders rather than the traditional powdered sugar. Leftovers also taste great in natural yogurt or smoothies, adding extra flavor at the same time.

APPLESAUCE

☞ *MAKES APPROX*
3½ CUPS, OR
4 JARS

2¼lb (1kg) apples, such as Fuji
(roughly 6 apples)

2–3 drops vanilla extract

pinch of ground cinnamon

Add the chopped apples to a pan with the vanilla extract, cinnamon, and ½ cup of water and bring to a boil. Reduce the heat, cover, and simmer the apples for about 10 minutes, until soft. Purée, pour into sterilized screw-top jars while still hot, and seal with the lids. The applesauce will keep for about 3 months if stored in a cool, dark place.

🖐 *10 MINS*   ⊟ *10 MINS*

COCONUT YOGURT

☞ *MAKES 4 CUPS*
YOGURT

4 cups coconut milk
(60–70 percent coconut
extract)

1 tbsp cornstarch

pinch of freeze-dried yogurt
cultures (powder)

Bring the coconut milk and cornstarch to a boil in a pan, stirring constantly, and simmer for 1 minute until thickened. Leave to cool to 100.4°F (38°C), then stir in the yogurt cultures. Pour into sterilized screw-top jars or into the containers in a yogurt maker and seal with the lids. Leave to stand for 12 hours in a warm location or in your yogurt maker. Let the yogurt rest in the fridge for at least 1 day. As the yogurt matures, it will gradually set more firmly. It will keep in a sealed container in the fridge for at least 7 days.

🖐 *10 MINS*   ❄ *1 DAY*   🌙 *12 HRS*

COCONUT CREAM

☞ *MAKES ABOUT
1½ CUPS*

1 × 15oz (400ml) can coconut
  milk (70 percent coconut
  extract)
1–2 drops vanilla extract

A day in advance, put the canned coconut milk in the fridge to chill for 24 hours. Remove and skim off just the solid coconut fat; the coconut water can be used in other recipes (for example, in smoothies). Beat the coconut fat and vanilla extract in a bowl for 3–5 minutes, until you have a creamy, fluffy consistency. Chill the coconut cream for 5–10 minutes before use.

5 MINS   ❄ *5–10 MINS*

CASHEW ICING

☞ *FOR 1 CAKE—
MAKES ¼ CUP*

BASIC RECIPE

1 tbsp cashew butter
2 tbsp almond milk
  (unsweetened)
1 tsp maple syrup
1–2 drops vanilla extract

COLORED VERSIONS

in addition to the basic recipe
1 tsp almond milk
  (unsweetened)
1–2 tsp fruit powder

Stir all the ingredients in a small bowl until smooth; the result should be a creamy icing.

For colored versions, add a fruit powder and, if necessary, stir an additional 1 teaspoon of almond milk into the icing.

5 MINS

BAKING TIPS, PANS, AND CONVERSION TABLE

We generally cook our recipes using the **nonconvection** oven setting. The fan tends to dry cakes out too much and is particularly unsuitable for sponge cake recipes. If your oven is somewhat older, it would be worth acquiring a digital oven thermometer.

While we use size M **organic eggs** for our cakes, the recipes specify the more common size L; use what's easiest for you. Butter and eggs should be kept at room temperature for perfect baking results. If you need to separate eggs, however, this is easiest if they are cold. To make sure the egg whites get really stiff when you beat them, use a ceramic or stainless-steel mixing bowl and wipe both the bowl and the whisk blades with some vinegar. This removes any fat residues and ensures the whites become properly stiff.

Coconut oil that has solidified can be melted in a pan over low heat before being added to your recipe. If your cake mix includes a flour that contains gluten, this should be mixed in only briefly. Stirring for too long will result in the mixture becoming too sticky, and the CO_2 bubbles will be too big. The mixture won't rise properly, and the end result will be heavy.

Over time, we have gradually acquired durable, carbon steel **baking pans**, such as Le Creuset, and cast aluminum bakeware with excellent heat conduction properties and a nonstick coating. The investment pays off because if you take care of the pans and wash them by hand, they will last a lifetime. We used the following pans for the recipes in this book:

- Round ceramic ovenproof dish (diameter $9^1/_2$in/24cm)
- Small springform pan (diameter 8in/20cm)
- Large springform pan (diameter $10^1/_2$in/26cm)
- Small bundt cake pan (diameter $5^1/_2$in/14cm)
- Large bundt cake pan (diameter $8^1/_2$in/22cm)
- Bundt cake/pudding basin (diameter $6^1/_4$in/16cm) with internal tube
- Muffin pan (with $2^1/_4$in/5.5cm diameter cups)
- Tartlet pans (diameter 4in/10cm)
- Tart pan (diameter 12in/30cm)
- Enamel baking sheet ($12^3/_4 \times 15^3/_4$in/33 × 41cm)
- Brownie pan ($8^1/_4 \times 8^1/_4$in/20.5 × 20.5cm)
- Loaf pan ($4^1/_2 \times 10$in/11 × 25cm)

If you don't have a particular baking pan, use a recipe conversion: multiply each ingredient by the factor from this table. For eggs, round the number up and use size S. You may need to alter the cooking time, so always test the cake is done by inserting a toothpick.

		☞ BAKING PAN SIZE AS PER RECIPE									
		Round pans (diameter in in/cm)									
		5/12	$6^1/_4$/16	7/18	8/20	$8^1/_2$/22	$9^1/_2$/24	$10^1/_2$/26	11/28	12/30	$12^1/_2$/32
NEW BAKING PAN SIZE	**5/12**	-	0.6	0.4	0.4	0.3	0.3	0.2	0.2	0.2	0.1
	$6^1/_4$/16	1.8	-	0.8	0.6	0.5	0.4	0.4	0.3	0.3	0.3
	7/18	2.3	1.3	-	0.8	0.7	0.6	0.5	0.4	0.4	0.3
	8/20	2.8	1.6	1.2	-	0.8	0.7	0.6	0.5	0.4	0.4
	$8^1/_2$/22	3.4	1.9	1.5	1.2	-	0.8	0.7	0.6	0.5	0.5
	$9^1/_2$/24	4.0	2.3	1.8	1.4	1.2	-	0.9	0.7	0.6	0.6
	$10^1/_2$/26	4.7	2.6	2.1	1.7	1.4	1.2	-	0.9	0.8	0.7
	11/28	5.4	3.1	2.4	2.0	1.6	1.4	1.2	-	0.9	0.8
	12/30	6.3	3.5	2.8	2.3	1.9	1.6	1.3	1.1	-	0.9
	$12^1/_2$/32	7.1	4.0	3.2	2.6	2.1	1.8	1.5	1.3	1.1	-

PRODUCT INFORMATION

Here, we provide an overview of the ingredients we use to
help make your baking healthier and more natural.

Organic certification

Not all organic products are equal. For instance, according to consumer advisers, the seal of approval from some associations, such as the Biodynamic Association, generally impose stricter requirements than the European certifications. This applies in particular to animal welfare and food processing. These official seals require that animals are kept in appropriate conditions and fed correctly. So cows are given only small amounts of concentrated feed, and their primary fodder is grass and hay. The guidelines for additives in the fodder are also more stringent, and the animals can be treated with antibiotics only in exceptional cases. Also, there may be minimal additives when processing foods.

1. FLOUR, BAKING POWDER, AND YEAST

Buckwheat flour

Like teff, buckwheat is a gluten-free pseudocereal. The flour is ground from the whole grain and has a delicate nutty flavor. As well as being rich in iron, buckwheat flour contains particularly high levels of protein and vitamins E, B1, and B2, as well as potassium, calcium, and magnesium. For lighter and moister baking results, buckwheat flour should ideally be combined with cornstarch, other types of flour, or ground nuts. You will find buckwheat flour in well-stocked supermarkets, organic stores, and health-food stores.

Spelt flour

Spelt is one of the oldest original types of cereal, and our current wheat varieties have been developed from this grain. It is rich in vitamins and minerals and can sometimes be consumed by people with a wheat intolerance—even though spelt is a type of wheat. This grain contains gluten and plenty of healthy nutrients, including all eight essential amino acids. It has a total protein content of 11 percent. The whole grain contains phosphorous, vitamins (especially certain B vitamins), silica, zinc, magnesium, manganese, iron, potassium, and copper. The high fiber content ensures you feel full for longer. Spelt is excellent for baking and can be used like wheat.

Spelt flour

This is the darkest of the ground spelt flour varieties. It has a hearty flavor and is good for yeasted doughs. It also contains lots of minerals, vitamins, and fiber from the outer hull of the spelt grain—and therefore contributes to a healthy diet.

Whole-grain spelt flour

Whole-grain spelt flour is ground using all parts of the cleaned grain and therefore contains even more fiber, minerals, trace elements, and vitamins than standard spelt flour. Depending on the recipe, we use whole-grain spelt flour by itself or in combination with other varieties of flour.

Einkorn flour

The ancient grain einkorn, which stems from wild wheat, has a nutty flavor and a high proportion of carotenoids, which give einkorn products a golden color. It also contains higher than average levels of lots of minerals and proteins. Einkorn contains gluten and the flour is relatively coarse, similar to semolina in consistency, which gives cakes a beautiful crisp texture. You will find einkorn flour in well-stocked organic stores and health-food stores, as well as from some online retailers such as Amazon.

Whole-grain emmer flour

Emmer is an almost forgotten variety of wheat that has a robust, nutty flavor. Organic farmers are now cultivating it once again for one important reason: thanks to its robust outer layer and dark color, emmer is highly resistant to damage from pests and sunlight. It has a high proportion of proteins, carotenoids, zinc, and magnesium. You will find whole-grain emmer flour in well-stocked supermarkets, organic stores, and health-food stores; it is also available from online retailers.

Almond flour

Almond flour has a delicate, nutty flavor and is produced by carefully grinding partially de-oiled almonds. This gluten-free flour is rich in protein, dietary fiber, calcium, and magnesium. It contains just 8–15 percent oil, which is 25 percent less than ground almonds. This makes it a very dry flour, allowing it to absorb moisture readily. As a result, it ensures your baking results are wonderfully moist. You will find almond flour in health-food stores and organic stores, and from online retailers.

Oats

Oats develop in the form of multiple branching panicles and are one of the healthiest cereals. Oats are produced from the entire grain, so they contain lots of fiber, protein, antioxidants, polyphenols, unsaturated fatty acids, and minerals such as magnesium, phosphorous, and zinc along with valuable vitamins. Of all the grains, oats have the highest amount of vitamins B1 and B6 and are one of the most useful sources of iron. Oats are not related to wheat and are thus gluten-free. However, it is recommended that people affected by celiac disease should consume only oats that are clearly labeled as "gluten-free." These varieties are specially cultivated, processed, and checked, so they can be guaranteed to be free from gluten contamination.

Oat flour

You will find oat flour in well-stocked organic stores. Alternatively, you can easily make it yourself from oats. Simply grind the oats in a food processor to create flour.

Chickpea flour

Chickpea (or gram) flour is a gluten-free flour made from hulled, finely ground chickpeas. Its sweet and nutty flavor makes it ideal for sweet recipes, as well as for making falafel and hummus. This relatively dry flour retains liquids well and ensures your cakes are beautifully moist. It scores well in terms of valuable dietary fiber and has a high protein content; the minerals iron, magnesium, and zinc; and the vitamins folic acid, B1, and B6. You will find it in well-stocked supermarkets, Asian stores, and organic stores.

Rye flour

Rye flour contains lots of valuable components from the outer hull of the grain, which means that fiber and minerals are retained in the end product. This grain contains gluten and a high proportion of minerals, particularly potassium and phosphorous, and supplies important amino acids. It also includes B-complex vitamins and vitamin E. Rye flour is excellent for using in both sweet and savory baking.

Teff flour

Teff is a gluten-free pseudocereal, also known as lovegrass. The flour is always ground from the unhulled whole grain, which gives it a nutty flavor. Teff is rich in iron, magnesium, calcium, essential fatty acids, and complex carbohydrates. Teff flour is particularly good for baking because it retains moisture and helps the end result keep for longer. We recommended combining cornstarch with teff flour to produce a lighter and fluffier texture. You will find teff flour in well-stocked supermarkets, organic stores, and health-food stores.

Polenta

Polenta is cornmeal that has been produced using the whole maize kernel. This traditional Italian ingredient tastes fabulous in sweet recipes and pastries.

Cornstarch

This culinary starch is derived from corn and is both gluten and lactose-free. When combined with flour, cornstarch gives cakes a lighter consistency. With powdered sugar, it is also used to help stabilize cream (in place of the less commonly found cream stiffener). You will find cornstarch in well-stocked supermarkets and organic stores.

Baking powder

Organic baking powder consists of cream of tartar (potassium bitartrate), baking soda, and cornstarch and works as an excellent rising agent for baking. It is phosphate-free, gluten-free, and vegan.

Active dried yeast

Yeast is used as a leavening agent for bread, causing the dough to rise and giving it a soft, fluffy texture. Unlike instant yeast, active dried yeast needs to be dissolved in water before being added to the other ingredients.

2. SWEETENERS

Maple syrup

The trunk of the North American maple tree contains a sweet sap that can be tapped off by drilling small holes and then boiled down to create a syrup. This is a natural product with no added substances. It is graded depending on its quality. Grade A is the first sap of the harvest: the syrup is pale, clear, and has a mild flavor. Grade C flows from the tree somewhat later: the syrup is darker and has a stronger flavor. Maple syrup has a caramel flavor with a subtle sweetness. When purchasing, we recommend high-quality, organic brands—which guarantee that the contents are 100 percent pure maple syrup, free of any chemicals or pesticides—instead of commercial nonorganic brands.

Dates

Dried dates are a purely natural product. Medjool dates have a juicy consistency and a subtle flavor rather like honey. Deglet Nour dates are more common and easier to find. They are slightly firmer and have a more floury texture, their skin is tougher, and they are easier to process. Dates are rich in sugar, so they have a high calorie content. But thanks to the fiber, potassium, calcium, magnesium, tryptophan, iron, and B vitamins they contain, they are still a good choice as a healthy snack. In cake mixtures, dried fruits can be used as a natural sugar substitute.

Honey, organic

Forest honey, light honey, canola honey—this natural product is available in a range of different versions, both single origin and mixed, produced organically or conventionally. The criteria for organic honey are stringent. They range from the bee-keepers' working methods to the way in which the animals are kept. The beehives must be made exclusively from natural materials. Within 2 miles (3km) of the hives, the pastures over which the bees range must contain only wild plants or land that is being farmed organically. This same area must not contain any incineration plants or factories emitting pollutants, or any highways. As winter fodder, the bees are to be given primarily their own honey and pollen. The wings of the queen must not be clipped. The honey must be processed carefully, avoiding any potential heat damage by ensuring that the temperature in the hive does not exceed 104°F (40°C). When harvesting the honey, it is not permitted to use chemical substances to keep the bees away. It is also prohibited to use drug treatments to combat parasites or disease. When purchasing, you should take care to note whether the honey originates locally or was produced in the US or has been imported. We always use locally produced organic honey.

Dark brown sugar

Dark brown sugar is a combination of white sugar and molasses; it is produced from cane sugar and contains all the minerals from the sugar cane juice. Its strong, distinctive flavor has hints of caramel or treacle. Dark brown sugar contains more molasses than light brown sugar, leading to a deeper color and more intense flavor. We prefer to use dark brown sugar from fair trade sources where farmers are paid higher prices and there is support for environmental and social projects. You will find dark brown sugar in well-stocked supermarkets, organic stores, and health-food stores.

3. DAIRY PRODUCE AND EGGS

Eggs, organic

We typically use organic eggs from free-range hens, size M (though for the recipes in this book, we have specified size L due to availability). It is important to us that animals are kept in good conditions and are well looked after and that sustainable methods are used on agricultural land. That's why we like to use organic eggs from laying hens where the male chicks are not gassed or culled after hatching for profit reasons. Instead, they are allowed to mature into adult chickens in good living conditions. These eggs cost a bit more in comparison to other organic eggs, which support the rearing of the male chicks.

Yogurt

As with milk, for animal welfare reasons, we like to use yogurt that has been produced organically and certified by the Soil Association. Organic natural yogurt made using cow's milk, goat's milk, or sheep's milk can be found in well-stocked supermarkets and organic stores. Alternatively, you can also make our recipes using lactose-free, unsweetened yogurt made from soy, almond, or coconut.

Yogurt cultures

Yogurt cultures consist of a combination of *Lactobacilli* specifically for producing yogurt or fermented milk products. Choosing a suitable yogurt culture is crucial for the taste and texture of the end product. This will determine whether the flavor of the yogurt is mild or more traditionally acidic. A yogurt culture containing the bacteria *Streptococcus thermophilus* and *Lactobacillus bulgaricus* will produce a "classic" yogurt—that is, set firm and with a strong flavor. For a more mellow yogurt, a culture without *Lactobacillus bulgaricus* is usually used. Probiotic yogurt can be created using *Lactobacillus acidophilus*. You will find yogurt cultures in health-food stores, pharmacies, or from online retailers such as The Kefir Company.

Coconut milk

Coconut milk is creamy, has a sweet flavor, and melts beautifully in the mouth. It is derived from the flesh of the coconut, which is finely ground with water, then filtered. The coconut content in the product varies: for making yogurt, you should use coconut milk with 60–70 percent coconut content; for coconut cream, use one with 70 percent. In vegan cooking, the latter is a popular choice as a cream substitute.

Almond milk

To make gluten- and lactose-free almond milk, the almonds are first roasted, then ground to a powder. This powder is then combined with water in a particular ratio and mixed thoroughly. This is followed by a resting phase, during which the mixture infuses and acquires its milky consistency before finally being strained. We prefer to use unsweetened organic almond milk with no additives, emulsifiers, or preservatives—just almonds, water, and sea salt. You will find organic almond milk in well-stocked supermarkets, health-food stores, and organic stores.

Milk, organic

Not all milk is the same. We prefer fresh, organic milk because of the emphasis on animal welfare. Farms have high standards for animal husbandry, including the quality of the pasture and animals having direct access to an exercise area, which strengthens their immune systems. Organically produced whole milk also contains more healthy omega-3 fatty acids and conjugated linoleic acid because the animals are predominantly fed on fresh grass or hay. The animals are not given any GM fodder or routine courses of antibiotics. Other milk options include organic fresh sheep's milk or goat's milk, which are mainly available from health-food stores. *See also* coconut milk, almond milk, and other plant-based milks.

Plant-based milk

Plant-based and lactose-free milk can be produced using soy, rice, oats, spelt, almonds, hazelnuts, cashews, macadamias, hemp, coconut, and lupin. For people who are allergic to nuts, the nut-free varieties should be used. Take care when purchasing to choose unsweetened products that do not contain any additives or emulsifiers. Some plant-based milks can also be made yourself. (You'll find any number of useful instruction guides online.)

Quark, organic

Exactly as with milk, for animal welfare reasons, we like to use organic quark. Organic low-fat quark and organic full-fat quark with 20 percent or 40 percent fat content (made using cow's milk, goat's milk, or sheep's milk) can be obtained from well-stocked supermarkets and health-food stores.

4. BUTTER AND FAT

Butter, organic

In the US, most butter is the standard yellow "sweet cream" butter, which is either salted or unsalted. Unlike margarine, which was invented only in the 19th century, butter is a natural product with a long tradition. Organic butter is often paler than conventionally produced butter, which can be colored using the additive beta carotene (E160a). Butter contains vitamins A, E, and K, plus iodine and selenium. Organic butter is better than conventionally produced butter in terms of the proportion of healthy fatty acids it contains (just like its source ingredient, organic milk). The proportion of lactose contained in cultured butter is also very low because it is largely eliminated thanks to the lactic acid bacteria, so people with a lactose intolerance are more likely to be able to consume this butter. If consumed in moderation, there are no health reasons to avoid using butter. At any rate, butter is preferable to margarine, which often contains hydrogenated fats, artificial additives, flavorings, soy, or palm oil, which is responsible for the destruction of rainforests.

Coconut oil

Coconut oil is produced from fully ripe coconuts using a mechanical cold pressing technique, then carefully siphoned off. The end product can vary widely in quality, so we like to use organically cultivated, fairtrade, virgin coconut oil with no additives. This comes from sustainable, mixed cropping systems and is produced without deforestation or creating plantations. Mild coconut oil is particularly good for baking because it doesn't have a strong flavor of its own.

Olive oil, extra virgin

Olive oil is a vegetable oil produced from the fruit and pits of the olive. The labeling system is regulated in the US by the US Department of Agriculture: "extra virgin olive oil" means the product is of the highest quality and has a very low acidity of less than 0.8 percent. For baking, it is best to use olive oils that have a mild flavor.

Vegetable oils

In addition to butter, we like using high-quality vegetable oils, such as canola oil. This contains essential omega-3 fatty acids, which are often consumed in insufficient quantities.

5. SPICES AND OTHER INGREDIENTS

Old apple varieties (see also page 124)

Polyphenols belong to the family of phytochemicals, which are beneficial to health, with some already proven effective against cancer and cardiovascular disease. Large quantities are usually contained in the peel and pips of apples. Plants require these phytochemicals for their defense systems and to protect themselves against various pests. They have a clear impact on the color and taste of plant-based foodstuffs. Modern apple varieties have been cultivated to exclude these specific polyphenols in order to improve the aesthetics of the fruit, to prevent it from going brown rapidly after cutting, and to reduce acidity levels. This is precisely why so many of the apples currently available just taste sweet, with no acidity and minimal flavor. The proportion of polyphenols in apples is also linked to how well the fruit can be tolerated. People with an allergy to apples are more likely to be able to consume older apple varieties with higher polyphenol levels than the more modern cultivars. This is because polyphenols can deactivate apple allergens, preventing them from being absorbed by the body. In addition to this special characteristic, older apple varieties also have a higher proportion of healthy antioxidants, which are crucial for the human immune system to combat free radicals. So it's worth hunting out local farmers' markets or growers who are cultivating and selling old apple varieties such as Cox's Orange Pippin.

Flowers, edible (see also page 24)

Edible flowers are a fantastic way to decorate baked items without adding any extra calories. Before consuming, check whether the plants have been treated with chemicals. Store-bought ornamental plants will usually have been sprayed, so they are best avoided. In supermarkets, seasonal edible flowers are sometimes sold in the herb section. If you want to pick flowers yourself, always do this in the open countryside or use untreated flowers from your own garden to avoid pollution. It's important to pick them at the right time because wilted flowers will not be very aromatic. The best time to pick most varieties is on a sunny morning just as the flowers have opened. Pick young flowers just before you need them, as they wilt rapidly. If necessary, they can be kept fresh for a few hours in a bowl of cold water. Before use, remove the stalks and any green sepals. For many flowers, such as roses and Sweet Williams, only the petals are edible, so as far as possible, the stamen should also be removed. To get rid of any dirt or concealed insects, we advise carefully rinsing flowers in cold water. But don't rinse elderflowers; otherwise, the pollen, which is responsible for their flavor, will be washed away. In the winter months, dried flowers are ideal and can be obtained from well-stocked supermarkets; health-food stores such as Whole Foods; or from online retailers such as Amazon, Gourmet Sweet Botanicals, Melissa's Produce, The Chef's Garden, and Marx Foods.

Cashew butter

Organic cashew butter is made from 100 percent organic cashew kernels with no additives, emulsifiers, or stabilizers. As a result, the oil naturally contained in the product can sometimes rise to the surface, but the creamy consistency can be restored by stirring. Cashew butter has a delicate nutty flavor and is ideal for refining cakes and for use in vegan cooking. We use it to create our "cashew icing" (see page 193), which we use instead of sugar frosting.

Peanut butter

Peanut butter consists of 100 percent ground peanuts. Different versions are available: organic, unsalted, salted, and crunchy. Consumed in moderation, peanut butter is a good source of protein. It contains more unsaturated than saturated fatty acids and is also rich in fiber, potassium, antioxidants, zinc, magnesium, vitamin E, and niacin. For baking, we use smooth, unsalted, organic peanut butter that has no additives.

Fruit and vegetable powders

These powders are made from 100 percent ripe fruits or vegetables, which have first been freeze-dried and then ground without any additives. Available varieties include: blueberry, strawberry, raspberry, black currant, and beet powder. You can buy fruit powders from well-stocked health-food stores or online retailers such as Biovea.

Rose hips, dried

Rose hips are one of the fruits with the highest quantity of vitamin C. Other important nutrients they have include vitamins B1 and B2, vitamin E, provitamin A, niacin, and also flavonoids, fruit acids, and pectin. Rose hips are carefully dried whole and can be used in baking like other dried fruit. Dried rose hips with no additives can be bought online.

Cocoa

Cocoa powder with a high cocoa butter content ensures a better chocolate flavor. The effect of cocoa is similar to that of dark chocolate. We like to use fairtrade organic cocoa.

Cacao nibs

Cacao nibs are produced from cocoa beans—that is, from raw, unprocessed cocoa. The cocoa beans are hulled, broken into little pieces, and dried. Thanks to the fermentation and drying process, they retain all the benefits of the raw product, such as important nutrients, and they develop a bitter flavor. Cacao nibs are one of the original forms of cocoa and are ideal for baking. They can be found in well-stocked supermarkets, organic stores, and health-food stores.

Ground ginger

Ground ginger is made from 100 percent ginger root, which has been carefully dried and then ground to create a powder. The powder is not quite as intense as fresh ginger, but it can add a fresh, tangy flavor to baked items. Ground ginger is ideal for baking because it is so convenient, but if you prefer to use fresh ginger, you shouldn't substitute it on a 1:1 basis because fresh ginger has a much stronger taste. A good rule of thumb is to use 1 tablespoon of fresh grated ginger for every $1/2$ teaspoon of ground ginger.

Cardamom, green

Green cardamom is distinguished by its fresh, green pods that contain black seeds with an intense sweet and tangy flavor. Cardamom should be as fresh as possible when used because once it has been ground, it rapidly loses its flavor and the active ingredients deteriorate. So only open the green pods and grind the black seeds shortly before use. Green cardamom pods can be found in well-stocked supermarkets, Asian stores, and organic stores.

Jam

Jam usually consists of minimal fruit and lots of sugar. We either create jam with less sugar ourselves for quick consumption or we look for organic jams with at least 70 percent fruit content and that is produced using raw cane sugar or agave syrup. This kind of jam contains no refined white sugar. There are also organic jams available that are made from 100 percent fruit without any additional sugar.

Bay leaves

You will find fresh bay leaves in the vegetable aisle at well-stocked supermarkets or at your health-food store. For many recipes, you can use the dried variety of bay leaf instead.

Almond butter

Organic almond butter is produced from 100 percent organic almonds and is high in protein. The color of the product depends on whether blanched or unblanched almonds are used. Paler almond butter is purer and produced from blanched, unroasted almonds. Darker almond butter is produced from toasted, unblanched almonds and has a stronger flavor. White almond butter is less readily available and more expensive, so we tend to use the darker variety for baking.

Marzipan, organic

There are two varieties of this product available: vegan organic marzipan is produced using organic almonds and raw cane sugar. You can also buy honey marzipan, which contains organic honey in addition to almonds, but otherwise has no other additives or humectants. Organic marzipan is available from health-food stores.

Rose water

Rose water consists of an infusion of rose petals and water and will add a floral, exotic note to your baking. Take care when purchasing that the product is genuinely rose water that has been produced for culinary purposes using unsprayed rose petals. It can be found in well-stocked supermarkets, Asian stores, health-food stores, and online.

Powdered sugar

This can be used together with cornstarch to help stabilize and thicken creams, fillings, and icing. It is also dusted on top of desserts for decoration, as well as for a sugary boost.

Chocolate, dark

If consumed in moderation (about 2 tablespoons per day), dark chocolate with a minimum cocoa content of 70 percent provides a healthier alternative to milk chocolate. It causes only gradual fluctuations in blood sugar levels, which in turn prevents hunger pangs and significantly reduces the risk of consuming unnecessary calories. This kind of chocolate also inhibits the release of stress hormones and therefore has a calming effect. The phytochemicals it contains, such as flavonoids, have a positive impact on the cardiovascular system. In addition, antioxidants protect the body's cells against free radicals and have anti-inflammatory properties. Dark chocolate can be either entirely or almost lactose-free depending on its milk content. As a consequence, people with a lactose intolerance are more likely to be able to consume dark chocolate than milk chocolate. Many varieties of dark chocolate are also vegan. We prefer to use fairtrade, organic dark chocolate.

Dried fruit
When buying dried fruit, always ensure the fruit is unsulfured and unsweetened. Dried fruit is a healthier alternative to other sweet treats. It contains no fat, but has plenty of nutrients and fiber. However, due to the high sugar and calorie content, dried fruit should be enjoyed only in small quantities. One of the recommended five daily portions of fruits and vegetables may be consumed in dried form. Dried fruit also adds a natural sweetness to baked items.

Vanilla, extract
Vanilla extract comes from the vanilla bean and is produced by infusing, or macerating, the bean in water or alcohol. Just a small amount can add a wonderfully mellow, sweet flavor to your cake, drink, or dessert. Alternatively, our recipes can always be made using the freshly scraped seeds from a vanilla bean.

Cinnamon
There are two types of cinnamon: cassia and ceylon. Most cinnamon sold in the US is cassia, with ceylon available from specialty online suppliers. We prefer to use ceylon cinnamon, which is more refined and has a more subtle flavor than cassia cinnamon and contains comparatively little coumarin: a flavoring that occurs naturally in cinnamon and which should be consumed only in moderation. Organic ceylon cinnamon is obtained exclusively from the bark of the ceylon tree and is cultivated organically. It has a delicately spicy flavor, which also adds to the impression of sweetness in baked items.

A

almonds
Berry ice cream cake — 47
"Elisenlebkuchen" — 176
Spiced honey "lebkuchen" — 182
Strawberry and almond cake — 55
Strawberry and almond muffins — 38
apples — 12, 15
Apple cake — 127
Apple crumble muffins — 128
Apple tart — 19
Apple waffles — 60
Applesauce — 192
Blackberry and apple pie — 130
Mini fruit pies — 159
Oat muffins — 42–43
Scones — 160
apricots
Apricot tart — 74
Carrot cake — 27

B

baking pans — 195
baking tips — 195
bananas
Banana bread — 166–167
Berry ice cream cake — 47
Oat muffins — 42–43
"Save a banana" pancakes — 115
beets
Beet bundt cake — 163
Beet cake — 172
berries
Berry pizza — 108
Late summer berry gateau — 95
see also blackberries; blueberries; cranberries;
gooseberries; raspberries; strawberries
blackberries
Berry ice cream cake — 47
Blackberry and apple pie — 130
Blackberry bundt cake — 91
Blackberry cheesecakes — 105
Blackberry Swiss roll — 102
Quince rye cake — 147
Raspberry and blackberry cobbler — 80
blueberries
Berry ice cream cake — 47
Blueberry "franzbrötchen" — 120
Blueberry galette — 101
Blueberry naked cake — 107
Blueberry pancakes — 85

Oat muffins — 42–43
bundt cakes
method — 76–77
recipes — 28, 91, 116, 123, 148, 163

C

carrots
Carrot cake — 27
Carrot cake swirls — 20
Oat muffins — 42–43
cherries
Cherry bundt cake — 28
Cherry hot cross buns — 31
Cherry tart — 79
Scones — 160
Stone fruit crumble — 71
Vanilla tartlets — 68
chickpeas
Chickpea pancakes — 138
Peanut blondies — 41
chocolate — 201–203
Beet cake — 172
Brownies — 168
Buckwheat bundt cake — 123
Double chocolate muffins — 32
Elderberry gateau — 111
Mini chocolate cakes — 134
Peanut blondies — 41
coconut
Coconut cream — 193
Coconut yogurt — 192
colorings, natural — 190–191
cranberries
Buckwheat bundt cake — 123
Cranberry cake — 185
Mini fruit pies — 159
Oat muffins — 42–43
currants
Black currant spirals — 92
Spring sheet cake — 52
see also red currants

D

dates — 198
Banana bread — 166–167
Berry ice cream cake — 47
Cherry tart — 79
Couronne — 179
Mini chocolate cakes — 134
Red currant teff cookies — 51

E

elderflowers and berries
Elderberry gateau 111
Strawberry and almond muffins 38
Teff waffles 44

F·G

figs
Fig and walnut bars 165
Upside-down cake 143
gooseberries
Crumble flatbreads 73
Yogurt cake 63
grains 12–13
Grape calzone 141

H·I·K

hazelnuts
Blueberry naked cake 107
Hazelnut bundt cake 116
Panettone 181
Red currant teff cookies 51
Upside-down cake 143
ingredients 196–203
kidney beans: Brownies 168

N

nuts
Banana bread 166–167
Cashew icing 193
Oat muffins 42–43
Zucchini cake 36
see also almonds; hazelnuts; peanut butter; walnuts

O

oats 197
Oat muffins 42–43
Oat waffles 82
Stone fruit crumble 71
organic products 13, 196

P

Parsnip cake 155
peanut butter 201
Peanut blondies 41
Pear and walnut bundt cake 148
plums

Buckwheat muffins 67
Crumble flatbreads 73
Plum and poppy seed tart 137
Plum cake 119
Stone fruit crumble 71

Q·R

quinces
Quince galettes 151
Quince rye cake 147
Raisin bread 133
raspberries
Berry ice cream cake 47
Mini chocolate cakes 134
Oat muffins 42–43
Raspberry and blackberry cobbler 80
Ricotta cheesecake 89
Spring sheet cake 52
Victoria sponge cake 59
red currants
Red currant teff cookies 51
Vanilla tartlets 68
Yogurt cake 63
rhubarb
Rhubarb tartlets 22
Spring sheet cake 52

S

Scones 160
seasonal products 13, 15, 188–189
soft cheese
Blackberry cheesecakes 105
Ricotta cheesecake 89
Spelt waffles 97
Squash muffins 171
strawberries
Spring sheet cake 52
Strawberry and almond cake 55
Strawberry and almond muffins 38
sugar 11–12

W·Z

walnuts
Apple tart 19
Couronne 179
Fig and walnut bars 165
Pear and walnut bundt cake 148
"Save a banana" pancakes 115
Squash muffins 171
Zucchini cake 36

ABOUT THE AUTHORS

Carolin Strothe is a photographer, art director, food stylist, and author. She was born in the historic town of Celle, Germany. She trained for 3 years as a professional photographer and studied communication design in Hannover, with a particular emphasis on visual communication. In parallel to her studies, she founded her own creative studio in 2004. This enabled her to work on a freelance basis on various editorial and corporate design projects for agencies such as Scholz & Friends and fischerAppelt. For over 6 years, she has been developing recipes for magazines and food manufacturers. Her work as a photographer and food stylist has been published in magazines such as *Better Photography*, *Thrive*, and *ORIGIN*. Since 2013, she has been writing the food blog "Frau Herzblut," which was recognized at the German Food Blog Contest (1st prize, Passion & Innovation).

Her husband, **Sebastian Keitel**, is a brand strategist, user experience designer, and lecturer in Interaction Design. He was born in the Bauhaus town of Dessau, Germany. He studied information science in Salzgitter and Hannover. He has worked for creative agencies such as Publicis Pixelpark, Saatchi & Saatchi, DDB, Hirschen Group, and Heimat. In this role, he has been responsible for brands from the health, leisure, tourism, and food sectors. As a strategist and designer, he researches and examines different food and health trends. In a nonprofessional capacity, he has been interested in healthy nutrition and organic farming for several years.

Carolin Strothe and Sebastian Keitel have been working collaboratively as freelancers for brands such as Die Techniker, TUI, and Alnatura for over a decade. Both authors more or less grew up in the garden. As a consequence, they share a powerful love of nature and an appreciation for fine food. Both of these foodies love cooking healthy recipes together using seasonal produce. They are also partial to barista-quality coffee, bicycle rides, and the culture of the swing era. They have a passion for lindy hop dancing and popping swing records on the turntable at parties.

A HUGE THANK YOU

Our heartfelt thanks go to Jamie Oliver, the "godfather" of this book, for his kind and generous support. Without him, this book would never have been written. Thanks a lot, bro!

A special thank you must go to our mom and mother-in-law, Sabine Strothe, who was always on hand with help and advice, exceptional prop discoveries, and endless treasures from her garden.

For all things writing-related, sincere thanks go to the DK publishing team—Monika Schlitzer, Sarah Fischer, Natalie Knauer, Annemarie Heinel, and Caren Hummel.

We would like to thank Melanie Follmer from 3punktf (www.3punktf.de), who conjured up the most stunning hand-thrown pottery, and also Anke Treuter and Le Creuset (www.lecreuset.de) for the finest bakeware in the world. Heartfelt thanks also to Yoori Khoo, Sarah Alongi, Chris Nowak, Franziska Schlupski, Kristiane Adam, and Uwe Meilahn for our wonderful exchanges.

Particular thanks must go to our family, friends, and neighbors who repeatedly volunteered as recipe testers and gave us invaluable feedback.

Last but not least, thank you to Indigo florists for all the special requests and loans they agreed to, and to the Hahne orchard for helping define the apple varieties.

For DK UK

Translator Alison Tunley
Editor Claire Cross
US editor Kayla Dugger
Senior editor Kate Meeker
Editorial assistant Poppy Blakiston Houston
Senior art editor Glenda Fisher
Jacket designer Harriet Yeomans
Producer, pre-production David Almond
Senior producer Tony Phipps
Managing editor Stephanie Farrow
Managing art editor Christine Keilty

For DK Germany

Publisher Monika Schlitzer
Managing editor Caren Hummel
Project manager Anne Heinel
Production Sabine Huttenkofer, Stefanie Staat
Production coordinator Ksenia Lebedeva
Producer Dorothee Whittaker

Recipes and text Carolin Strothe, Sebastian Keitel
Photography and styling Carolin Strothe, Sebastian Keitel
Portrait of Jamie Oliver James Lyndsay

First American Edition, 2019
Published in the United States by DK Publishing
1450 Broadway, 8th Floor, New York 10018

Copyright © 2019 Dorling Kindersley Limited
DK, a Division of Penguin Random House LLC
19 20 21 22 23 10 9 8 7 6 5 4 3 2 1
001–314119–May/2019

A catalog record for this book is available from the Library of
Congress.
ISBN 978-1-4654-8395-9

Printed and bound in China

A WORLD OF IDEAS:
SEE ALL THERE IS TO KNOW

www.dk.com